Note

Whilst every effort has been made to ensure that the content of this book is as technically accurate and as sound as possible, neither the author nor the publishers can accept responsibility for any injury or loss sustained as a result of the use of this material.

Published by A & C Black Publishers Ltd
36 Soho Square, London W1D 3QY
www.acblack.com

First edition 2009

Copyright © 2009 Alun Richardson

ISBN 978 0 7136 8690 6

A CIP catalogue record for this book is available from the British Library.

own in
:yclable.
ironmental

ACKNOWLEDGEMENTS

The ideas in this book are the culmination of 25 years mountaineering and time spent discussing techniques with inspirational climbers, Mountain Guides and instructors, in particular Dave Williams, Steve Lewis, Graeme Ettle, Bruce Goodlad, Eric PirieTrevor Massiah, Clive Hebblethwaite, John Taylor, Twid Turner, Louise Thomas and Pat Littlejohn.

Special thanks to Lesley Jones who supported me throughout; Clive Hebblethwaite and Twid Turner who supplied some photographs; friends who posed for photographs – Trevor Massiah, Bas Jongmans, Paul Donnithorne, Clive Hebblethwaite, Paul Donnithorne, Emma Alsford and Gareth Richardson; Rhiannon Richardson and Molly Jones for help with text and diagrams; George Manley for his excellent illustrations; Robert Foss and Lucy Beevor from A&C Black and the manufacturers who generously supported the photo shoots: DMM, Lyon Equipment, Mountain Equipment, Face West, Select Solar, Mammut and Fritschi.

Any of the opinions expressed in this book are mine and should not be associated with any of the above people, companies or organisations.

'Rather than being a risk-taker, I consider myself, and my climbing peers to be risk-controllers, keeping risk at a reasonable level.'
　　　　　– Alex Lowe, one of the world's best climbers

Rock Climbing is the second book in the **Rucksack Guide** series and covers the skills and techniques required to become a competent rock climber. This handy book can be kept in your rucksack and will help you to gain the experience to climb safely anywhere in the world. **The Rucksack Guide** series tells you *what* to do in a situation, but it does not always explain *why*. If you want more information behind the decisions in these books, go to *Mountaineering: The Essential Skills for Mountaineers and Climbers* by Alun Richardson (A&C Black, 2008).

Rock climbing is hazardous, and there are always factors beyond your control. Safe climbing is having an awareness of the hazards and matching your skills and experience to the dangers to decrease the risks. Unfortunately, good judgement only comes with experience and, as Oscar Wilde said, 'Experience is simply the name we give to our mistakes', so always tread carefully!

For more about the author, his photographs and the mountaineering courses he runs go to:
　　www.alunrichardson.co.uk and
　　www.fredomphotographs.co.uk.

Understanding how forces are generated, how to lessen them and how to use climbing equipment will make you a safer climber.

THE KILONEWTON

A kiloNewton (kN) is a measurement of force. If you are hanging on a rope the force on the rope in kN is your mass divided by 100 (so a person weighing 80kg creates a force of 0.8kN).

IMPACT FORCE (IF)

- Impact force = the amount of energy a falling lead climber generates, reaching a maximum when the rope has fully stretched.
- IF is partly dissipated by dynamic elements in the system, e.g. stretched rope fibres, friction over karabiners, the movement of the belayer, knots tightening etc.
- The remaining energy is transmitted to the climber, the belayer/anchors and protection.
- The force transmitted to the protection is nearly doubled.

ROPES DON'T BREAK, THEY ARE CUT

'A rope used for normal climbing cannot break in a fall; however, its ability to hold a fall over an edge is dramatically reduced with time.'

(German Alpine Club (DAV))

If you don't trust it, get rid of it or downgrade a leading rope to top roping.

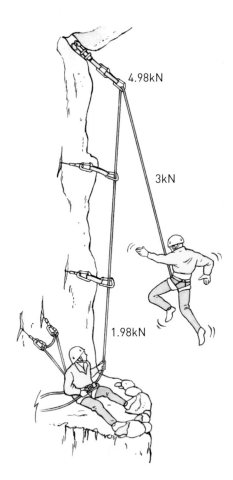

4.98kN

3kN

1.98kN

Fig. 1 Forces on a climber, belayer and equipment

FALL FACTOR (FF)

The severity of a fall can be approximated by the fall factor: the distance fallen divided by the amount of rope paid out, which ranges from zero to two. Zero equals no force on the rope and you have probably hit the ground! If a runner is placed at 2m the fall factor is halved.

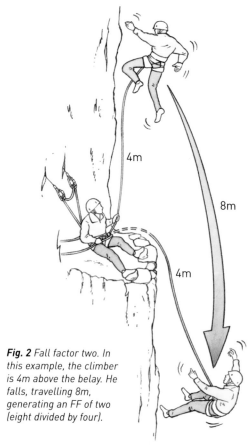

4m

8m

4m

Fig. 2 Fall factor two. In this example, the climber is 4m above the belay. He falls, travelling 8m, generating an FF of two (eight divided by four).

VECTOR FORCES

Loads begin to multiply alarmingly at angles greater than 120 degrees. Ensure the angle formed by the protection is 90 degrees or less (Fig. 3).

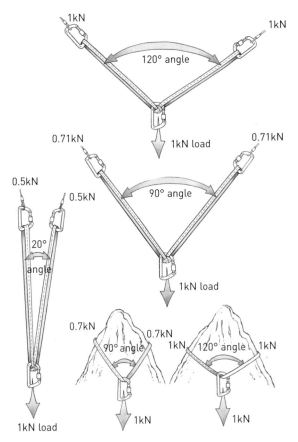

Fig. 3 *Vector forces*

- Keep knots neat and pull them snug, but not over-tight, because the tightening process absorbs energy.
- All knots should be tied leaving a tail at least 10 times as long as the diameter of the rope e.g. 11cm in an 11mm rope.

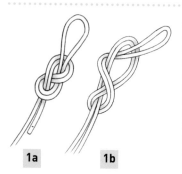

1a   **1b**

Fig. 4.1a and 4.1b Figure of eight on a bight. Usage: Tying into the rope; forming attachment points for belays. Difficult to adjust and undo after loading. The figure of nine (4.1b) takes an extra turn before finishing the knot, so is less likely to tighten.

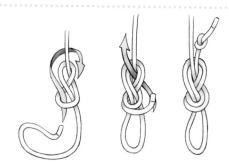

Fig. 4.2 Rewoven figure of eight. Usage: *Tying into the rope; connecting the rope to an anchor. Difficult to untie after loading, easy to see if it is tied incorrectly, does not come loose and is good at absorbing the forces generated in a fall. The rewoven overhand creates a smaller knot, but is difficult to untie.*

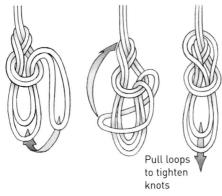

Pull loops
to tighten
knots

Fig. 4.3 Double figure of eight on a bight (bunny ears).
Usage: Limited use for linking two anchors at a belay.
Creates two loops adjustable to differing lengths. The
same knot created with an overhand knot can come
undone unless both ends remain clipped.

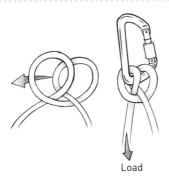

Load

Fig. 4.4 Clove hitch. Usage: A useful knot for attaching rope
to anchor krabs. Requires a load in each direction in order to
be effective and should not be relied on for use with slippery
rope, as it can become loose. However, this does make it
useful for adjusting the length of the running end.

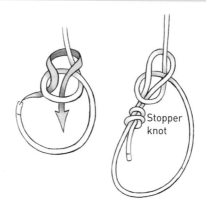

Fig. 4.5 Bowline with a stopper knot. Usage: *Commonly used to tie into a climbing harness. The bowline can come undone with movement, hence the stopper knot secures it.*

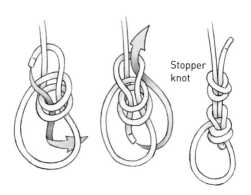

Fig. 4.6 Improved bowline. *Does not become loose as easily as the bowline knot in Fig. 4.5.*

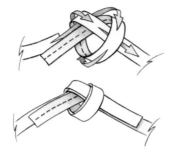

Fig. 4.7 Tape knot/water knot. Usage: For tying tapes or ropes together. This is not often used because of the invention of stitched slings. Do not stitch or tape the ends down.

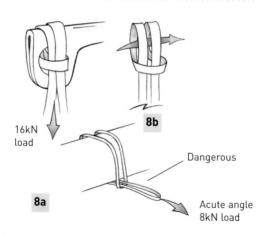

Fig. 4.8a and b The lark's foot/girth hitch. Usage: Safe and useful for attaching a sling to a harness and tying off a peg, but only when tied without an acute angle created by the sling (Fig. 4.8a), which may multiply the forces and, in exceptional circumstances, could break. A much misunderstood hitch.

KNOTS AND HITCHES

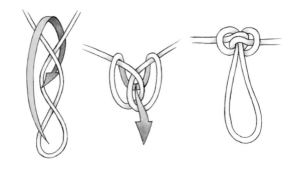

Fig. 4.9 Alpine butterfly. Usage: For tying into the middle of the rope and for equalising anchors. Useful for isolating a piece of damaged rope. Has the advantage over the figure of eight and overhand knot, because it directs the force through the knot and doesn't distort it.

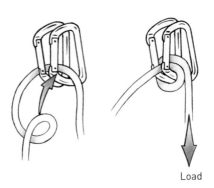

Load

Fig. 4.10 Garda/alpine hitch. Usage: Locks the rope so that it only moves in one direction. Can be used as part of a pulley system. Auto-locking hitch (use identical krabs).

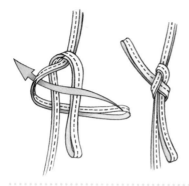

Fig. 4.11 Sheet bend. Usage: *Creates a chest harness called a Parisian baudrier. Very fast to tie and useful when attaching two ropes of different diameters.*

Fig. 4.12 Overhand on a bight. Usage: *Use in place of an alpine butterfly or figure of eight. Creates a small loop in a sling or rope, and is difficult to undo after loading, unless tied in a bunch or ropes of slings.*

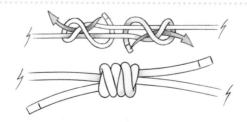

Fig. 4.13 Double fisherman/grapevine. Usage: *For tying two ropes together and the ends of cord on protection. Ensure that the two portions of the knot fit into each other. A triple fisherman's knot is used for tying Spectra and Dyneema cord.*

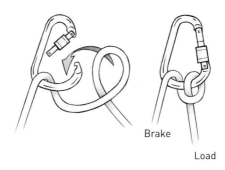

Brake

Load

*Fig. 4.14 Italian hitch/münter hitch. Usage: Easy to use
with an HMS krab for belaying and lowering moderate loads.
Really a half clove hitch as its German name 'halbmastwurf
sicherung' (HMS) indicates. Be careful that it does not untwist
the locking gate as the rope moves through the krab.*

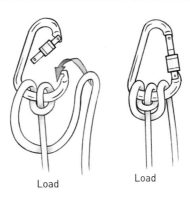

Load   Load

*Fig. 4.15 Super münter hitch. Usage: A beefed up version
of the münter hitch with two main advantages – it creates
friction, and it reverses the twist in the rope that the standard
münter creates, making the super münter best for lowering.*

Fig. 4.16 Slippery hitch/mule knot. *Usage: For tying off belay plates, as it is easily released. It holds securely as long as there is a load on the standing end.*

Fig. 4.17 French prusik/marchard hitch. *Usage: Most useful knot for protecting abseils (see Rescues, p. 72 for more information), as it ties a loop of rope to another rope and slides only in one direction.*

COMMUNICATION

- Keep calls to a minimum.
- Add the person's name when the crag is crowded.
- When communication is difficult, whistle – one whistle means safe.
- Rope tugs can be confusing – only climb when the rope is pulled very tight.

CLIMBING CALLS

1 When the leader has attached to the belay anchors, the shout *'Safe'* informs the second that they no longer have to belay the leader.

2 The second removes the rope from the belay device and shouts *'Take in'*. This tells the leader that they can pull the spare rope up and that the second has heard *'safe'* and taken them off belay.

3 When the rope comes tight, the second shouts *'That's me'*. This tells the leader that it is the second on the end of the rope and that the rope has not become jammed.

4 The leader puts the rope into the belay device and, when he is ready to take responsibility for the second, shouts *'Climb when ready'*.

5 The second starts to dismantle the anchors if on a multi-pitch climb (and not before) and shouts *'Climbing'*.

6 The leader acknowledges that they have heard the call by replying *'OK'*.

Learning to lead is exhilarating, yet daunting. There are methods you can use to make it less harrowing when starting out:

- **Gear pre-placement** Abseil down the climb and place protection prior to leading.
- **Bottom rope** Use a bottom rope belayed by your partner and drag your climbing rope behind you.
- **Fixed rope with loops** Simulate a more realistic leading situation by tying figure of eight knots or alpine butterflies into an abseil rope every 2m, with a quick draw attached. Remove some of the stretch using an Italian hitch on a ground belay. Climb with one half rope clipped into the quick draws and one single rope, that you clip into the gear you place.

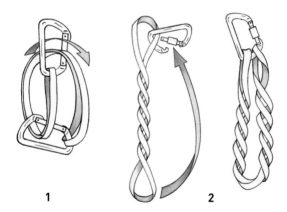

1　　　　　　　　　　　　**2**

Fig. 5 Two methods for shortening slings

ORGANISING CLIMBING GEAR

- Carry 8 nuts per krab, doubled up in size order.
- Distribute protection equally on either side of your harness.
- When lay-backing, carry the gear on the side away from the wall (a bandolier may help).
- Ensure spare screw gates are not done up.
- 60cm slings can be placed over the head or arm, but are difficult to remove (Fig. 5 shows alternative methods).
- Do not clutter your harness with a knife, jumars or cleaning rags.
- Carry a nut key, even when leading.

A TYPICAL RACK

6 quick draws (12 krabs and 6 short slings)
6 longer extenders (12 krabs and 6x60cm slings)
2 120cm slings and krabs
2 60cm slings and krabs
2 sets of wires 1–9
1 set of Wild Country Rockcentrics 5–9
6 camming devices
2 spare open gate krabs
3 screwgates
2/3 HMS krabs
1 nut key
1 belay device

TYING INTO A HARNESS

- Concentrate and check your partner.
- Never attach yourself to the rope using a locking krab.
- The rewoven figure of eight (Fig. 4.2, page 6) is the most reliable knot, but the improved bowline (Fig. 4.6, page 8) is easier to untie after loading.
- Take just over an arm's length of rope and tie a single figure of eight knot.
- Take the end down through the waist belt and leg loops.
- Re-thread the figure of eight to create a fist-sized central loop.
- Tie an overhand knot in the single strand that makes up the tail.

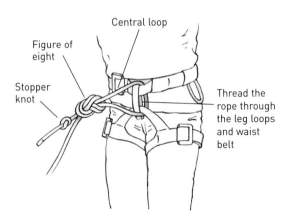

Central loop

Figure of
eight

Stopper
knot

Thread the
rope through
the leg loops
and waist
belt

Fig. 6 *Tying in (see also Fig. 4.2)*

Attach the belay device to the 'central loop' created by tying in (Fig. 7). Ensure the rope runs cleanly through the belay device without any twists. Use an HMS krab for smooth action, the wide end towards the belay device.

The upward movement of a belayer during a fall helps to absorb the force generated.

As long as the belayer is attentive there is no need to anchor them to the ground or the cliff, unless one or more of the following apply:

● The leader is more than 50 per cent heavier
● The belayer could fall off a drop
● The climb is threatened by waves
● There are many boulders to stumble over.

Having freedom of movement allows the belayer to move out of the way of falling objects.

A GOOD BELAYER...
● Does not rummage in a rucksack or smoke.
● Is positioned close to the cliff to keep the runners in place.
● Ensures that the ropes do not wrap around the leader's legs.
● Stands up – it is a more comfortable position to absorb the forces created by a fall.
● Pays out just enough rope – do not pull the climber backwards, but do not give too much rope.
● Loosely feeds the ropes on to the ground with the leader's end on top to avoid tangles.

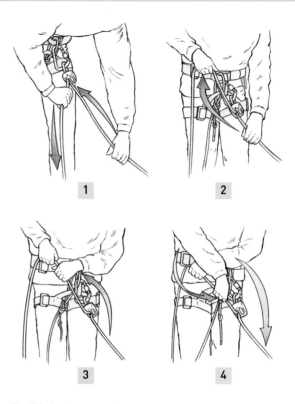

Fig. 7 Belaying a second using a belay tube

*1   Bring the live and dead ropes parallel and pull the
     live rope through.*

*2–4 Move the brake hand back and change hands – always
     have one hand on the dead rope throughout the
     changeover. To hold a fall, pull the brake hand
     backwards forcing the rope into a 'Z' shape and
     increasing the friction.*

USING OTHER BELAYING DEVICES

Italian hitch

The Italian hitch provides sufficient braking power no matter where your hand is. It is useful for 'direct belaying' a second, or 'indirect belaying' a leader, but avoid it when a long leader fall is likely. The action is the opposite of a belay plate – keep hands in front of the hitch at all times, which means that you do not have to be close to the hitch.

Gri Gri

When belaying a leader the rope can jam. Hold the auto-locking mechanism down with the thumb when paying the rope out (Petzl do not recommend this method). Hold the dead rope at all times – the release arm is an on-off switch and it is possible to drop the climber when lowering them.

Fig. 8 Belaying with a Gri Gri (note the use of a krab to add friction during a lower).

Locking belay devices

Keep hold of the dead end of the rope with the whole of your hand during the locking off process. Keep the belaying hand close to the device and use the other hand to do the knot tying (Fig. 9).

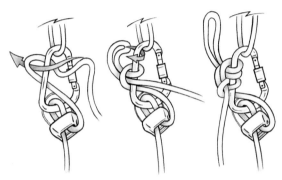

Fig. 9 *Locking a belay device*

Locking an Italian hitch

Pull approximately 60cm of rope forwards and secure it in front of the hitch with a slippery hitch and a half hitch around the live rope.

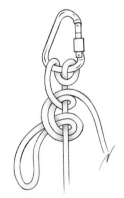

Fig. 10 *Tying off an Italian hitch*

The ideal belay at the top of a climb puts the belayer sideways to the anchors (p. 47), with the ropes along one side of the body. To ensure that the brake arm is free to move and lock the belay device, it should be on the same side as the ropes. Belaying can also be compromised by a second that climbs too fast, so tell them to slow down.

BELAYING TWO SECONDS

Belaying two seconds at the same time with a standard belay device requires dexterity. Instead, use an auto-locking device (Petzl Reverso) attached directly to the belay, because it allows both ropes to be locked independently (Fig. 11). The main disadvantage is that if both or even one climber falls off, it is difficult to lower them and the device must be unloaded (take care using them on overhanging rock). Take care when belaying climbers on half ropes, because there is a lot of stretch.

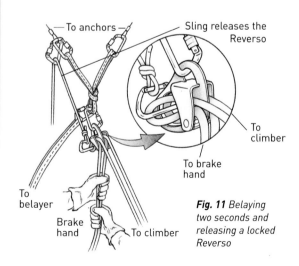

Fig. 11 Belaying two seconds and releasing a locked Reverso

DIRECT AND INDIRECT BELAYING

- A **direct belay system** transmits the forces in a fall direct to the belay anchors.
- An **indirect belay system** transmits the forces in a fall to the belay anchors via the belayer.
- A **semi-direct belay system** transmits the forces in a fall direct to the anchors, but by changing position the belayer also absorbs the force.

LOWERING

It is easier, smoother and more comfortable for the belayer to lower directly from the belay anchors (Fig. 12). To prevent the possibility of lowering off the end of the rope, tie the end into the belay anchors.

Two climbers can be lowered at the same time by tying one climber into the end of the rope and the other into an isolation loop two arm-spans away, created using an overhand knot or alpine butterfly.

Fig. 12 Lowering. To make it easier to control the belay device, take the dead rope through a krab above the belay device.

Choosing the appropriate protection and placing it quickly is an art. There are a number of reasons to place protection. It will:

- Reduce the fall factor
- Keep the rope in as straight a line as possible (Figs 22–4, pp. 38–40).
- Reduce the length of a fall due to fatigue, loose rock or a slip
- Help the second follow the route
- Protect the rope from sharp edges or loose rock.

CHOOSING SOUND ROCK

Runner placements are rarely perfect. When you have chosen a placement, look for cracks that may make the whole area loose. Place one hand on the rock and bang it with the palm of the other – if you feel a vibration, kick or pull the rock. Look for soft rock and crystals inside cracks that can wedge a runner, but can also snap easily in a fall.

Fig. 13 *A sling doubled over a spike and knotted allows the forces generated in a fall to be distributed over two strands of the sling, rather than just one.*

PLACING PROTECTION TIPS

- Identify possible placements before leaving the ground, organising them on your rack.
- Keep vital protection for the crux.
- Down-climb if necessary to retrieve protection that may be required higher up.
- Place the largest, properly fitting nut, and ensure that the maximum surface area is in contact with the rock.
- Place protection deep into a crack – not on the outside – but do not embed it so deeply that it cannot be retrieved.
- The distance between runners can increase the higher you climb.
- Do not focus on looking upwards; look sideways and downwards for placements.
- Place protection when you can.
- Do not rely on a single piece of gear unless it is perfect.
- Be suspicious of all fixed gear.
- Worry about the quality of the rock, not the strength of the equipment.
- Do not trust well-worn runner placements.
- When lay-backing, place gear at waist level to avoid becoming pumped.
- Clip bolts when they are at waist level – you are less likely to fall with a lot of slack rope.
- Double up small protection pieces.
- When the placement is out of reach, link two wires together.

PROTECTION

Nature provides some of the best protection requiring the simplest of equipment.

SPIKES AND BOULDERS
The strongest way to place a sling is to loop it around natural protection, either single or double (Fig. 13). Rope slings are better on sharp edges, but they can roll off rounded boulders. Roll the sling back and forth to ensure it is not going to come off the spike. Place the double thickness of the stitched portion over any sharp edges.

THREADS
Threads in solid rock can take a pull in any direction, making them one of the safest runners (Fig. 14). Thread a sling through a hole and clip with a krab. Even better, thread a sling through the hole, tie an overhand knot and pull the knot back into the thread tunnel. Any force from a fall is then on the knot, and not the rock neck. Do not lark's foot a sling around the neck. Wired runners can also be used as threads.

Fig. 14 *Threads*

CHOCKSTONES
Thread or lark's foot to the chockstone.

TREES
Avoid trees for environmental reasons, but if you do have to use one, ensure it is at least arm thickness, has vigorous growth and a deep, well-developed root system. Trees and bushes are more brittle after dry and cold weather. If the tree is used regularly, pad it, but remove the padding after use. Loop a sling around the tree at its base to reduce leverage, or tie the rope to it with a bowline.

NUTS AND WEDGES

The simplest protection after a natural runner. Most wedges above half an inch are designed with a complementary thickness-to-width ratio, i.e. the wider profile of a Rock 7 is the same as the narrow profile of a Rock 8. The most popular wedge-shaped nuts have curved sides so that they cam on the convex side and rotate into the best position. In hard rock the softer micro nuts can deform and pull out, whereas in soft rock brass micros have a better bite than harder nuts, which can shear through.

HEXENTRICS

More reliable than SLCDs (p. 29), hexentrics can also be used sideways as a wedge (Fig. 15). They fit into pockets and are useful in vertical and horizontal placements. They may move backwards when the crack is inwardly flaring.

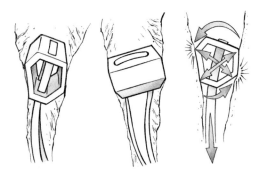

Fig.15 *Placing hexentrics, which jam into place when they twist.*

PROTECTION

PLACING SPRING-LOADED CAMMING DEVICES (SLCDS)

SLCDs can sit in poor placements, held by the small force generated by the spring. It is therefore vital that they are placed correctly:

- Place at 50 per cent of the expansion range with the stem in line with the direction of any forces applied.
- Beware of cracks that widen as they deepen.
- Ensure all the cams are in contact.
- Avoid cramming a cam into a small placement.
- Cams rotate – check the placement after a fall.

Horizontal placements:
- Place wider cams at the base for stability.
- Use flexible stemmed cams, because the stem flexes over the rock. (Although, even flexible cams still work best when aligned in the direction of force).
- Place rigid stemmed cams so that only a small amount of the bar is showing, or tie them off.

WARNING

Beware of tying off a rigid cam in front of the triggers, because a fall may release the cams. Instead, fit rigid Friends with a second sling through one of the holes designed for making the device lighter (Fig. 16B). They even hold with just three cams in contact with the rock.

!

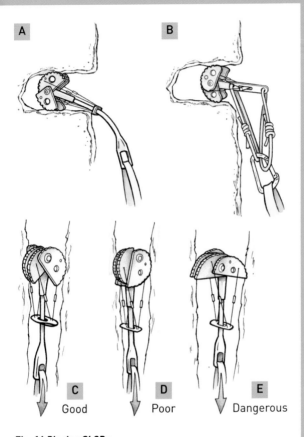

Fig. 16 Placing SLCDs
A *Flexible SLCDs are more versatile in horizontal placements.*
B *A tied-off rigid stem may transmit the load to the cams in a more predictable manner, but only when placed correctly.*
C *A perfect placement.*
D *Over-cammed, and will be difficult to remove.*
E *Under-cammed. It is now acting like normal passive protection.*

PROTECTION

TRI-CAMS
Useful in pockets and slots and can be used like a wedge. They are, however, unstable, can fall out if not well-seated and may need a tug to seat them in place.

SPRING-LOADED WEDGES
These work well in narrow, shallow, parallel cracks, but the placement is only as good as the purchase on the rock, and the holding power is reduced when fully extended.

Fig. 17 *Tri-cams work where nothing else can.*

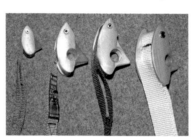

Fig. 18 *Sliding nuts all work on the same principle – a small spring-loaded wedge slides against the larger fixed wedge.*

SHARING THE LOAD
When each piece of protection is in a poor place-ment, connect them together to share the load and create a stronger piece. If you cannot tie a knot with one hand, use the self-equalising method described for slings (Fig. 19 and 33), but beware; if one comes out the other will be shock-loaded.

The force generated by a fall can exert a sideways or outward pull on runners, cams can invert and walk sideways and nuts placed in vertical and horizontal placements can lift out. Protection that takes a pull in any direction is therefore going to be better. Threads, trees and bolts and – to a lesser degree – pegs are multidirectional, but you can also link protection in opposition (Fig. 19).

REMOVING PROTECTION

- Avoid tugging violently – especially on micro wires.
- Loosen with a nut key and remove them the way they went into the rock.
- Do not move cams back and forth, as they can walk into the crack.
- Hook the bar using two wires or a specialist nut key if the trigger bar cannot be reached.
- Hook the cam with the nut key pick if the cam has a single finger trigger ring.
- Try hooking the holes in the cam itself.
- To prevent a piece of gear being dropped, clip the quick draw or extender into the gear loop of the harness before you remove it from the rope.

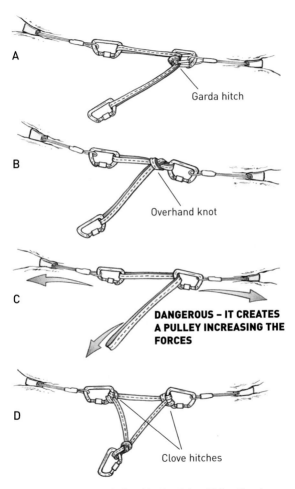

A

Garda hitch

B

Overhand knot

C

**DANGEROUS – IT CREATES
A PULLEY INCREASING THE
FORCES**

D

Clove hitches

Fig. 19 *Equalising vertical and horizontal multidirectional placements to prevent them being pulled out. Turn the diagram on its side to see vertical equalisation.*

Treat any fixed gear with caution – if you are in any doubt, replace it.

PLACING PEGS

A perfectly placed peg should:

- Slide one-third of the way in before hammering.
- Go all the way up to the eye when hammered.
- Have a rising ringing sound as you hammer it into the crack. (A dull 'clunking' sound usually indicates a poor placement).

If you are unable to hammer the peg all the way in, stop hammering to avoid loosening the peg. Tie it off using a slipknot, lark's foot or clove hitch (Fig. 20). The clove hitch will not come off the peg, but it puts the load further away from the rock. The slipknot comes undone, but places the load closest to the rock.

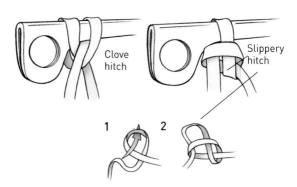

Fig. 20 Tying off pegs with a clove hitch and slippery hitch

TIPS

- Soft rock requires a soft peg, and hard rock a hard peg. A soft steel peg is better when the crack curves internally.
- The ideal peg placement should make an acute angle between the rock and the direction of the force exerted.
- Bend soft pegs that protrude to decrease the leverage.
- A horizontal placement is always better than a vertical one.
- In a vertical crack, make use of any variations in the rock to hold the piton in place; a narrowing above and below the peg is ideal to prevent the peg pivoting out.
- The eye of the peg is best placed downwards, horizontally.
- In roof cracks, place the longest peg possible with slight horizontal inclination.
- A peg placed in a three-way corner is almost impossible to remove!
- When using angles, place pegs with three points of contact.

TESTING PEGS

Without a hammer it is difficult to test a peg. Try loosely holding a krab with two fingers and tap it on the peg; the sound it makes will indicate whether it is safe.

REMOVING PEGS

Try gentler blows first in a predominantly upward direction because then a nut placement is created. However, in practice it is difficult to remove a peg with blows in only one direction. When it is loose attach a chain of krabs to it and pull outwards.

***Fig. 21** A wire through the eye helps with difficult-to-clip pegs.*

FIXED PROTECTION – BOLTS

- Beware of any bolt that is crooked, wobbles or is in loose or soft rock. Hammering bolts that do not tighten, are in too shallow a hole, or are stripped worsens the situation because the bolt is at risk of bending or cracking.

- Never smash a bolt flat. If it offends you and you need to remove it, pull it out using a thin flat piton with a 'V' cut into it and a crow bar. If the bolt breaks, punch the remaining stud as deep as possible.

- To remove glue in bolts, try twisting with a crow bar or cut and punch them in.

- To refill the holes, mix resin with rock dust or use rock-coloured cement.

ATTACHING THE ROPE TO PROTECTION

Use a quick draw or an extender to link the rope to runners. They act as a hinge, preventing the runner from lifting out. If you do have to use a single krab on bolts or pegs, use a screw gate. Keep the gates away from edges to prevent the gate being pushed open.

KEEPING THE ROPE IN A STRAIGHT LINE

The only runner that receives a downward force in a fall is the top one; the remainder receive outward pulls towards an imaginary straight line between the belayer and the climber (Fig. 22). Therefore, consider the direction that the force will apply to all runners, and not just the last one. Also consider the effect that a falling second will have on the protection, especially when traversing (Fig. 23).

Maintaining a straight line also allows the rope to effectively absorb the forces in a fall (Fig. 23), reducing rope drag (friction) and the IF (p. 2).

Use longer slings to straighten the rope and, when possible, the first runner should be able to take an outward or upward pull. In addition to extending the runners to keep the rope in a straight line, the belayer should stand close to the cliff.

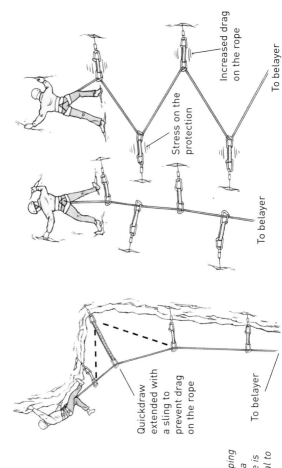

Increased drag on the rope

Stress on the protection

To belayer

To belayer

Quickdraw extended with a sling to prevent drag on the rope

To belayer

Fig. 22 *Keeping the rope in a straight line is fundamental to safety.*

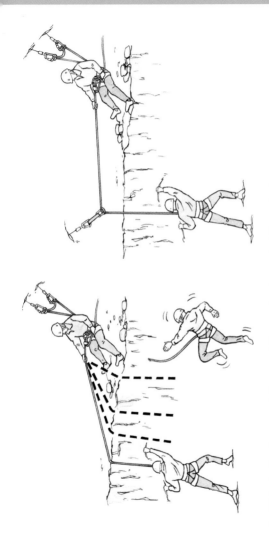

Fig. 23 Protecting the second. Beware of the rope tearing against the rock edge.

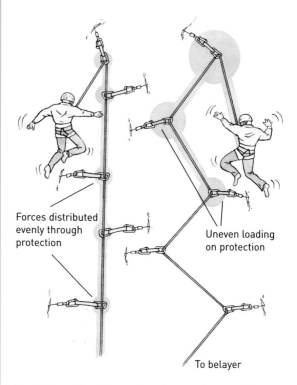

Forces distributed evenly through protection

Uneven loading on protection

To belayer

Fig. 24 *Absorption of forces keep the ropes in a straight line to absorb the forces generated by a fall.*

Fig. 25 Extend runners with a sling or another wire to prevent the krab breaking over an edge.

LOOK AFTER THE SECOND ON TRAVERSES
Protect the hard moves before and after the crux, even if you do not need protection – the second climber invariably removes the runner before making the difficult moves, and then faces a fall if you have not placed a runner. Consider placing protection for the second on vertical pitches that have a gradual or subtle traverse

CLIPPING THE ROPE INTO A QUICK DRAW
There are two ways of clipping the rope into a krab depending on the direction it is facing and which hand you are using (Fig. 26). The rope should pass from the back of the krab and out to the climber. When climbing diagonally, the gate of the krab should face away from the direction the climber is heading (Fig. 27).

PROTECTION

CLIPPING THE ROPE

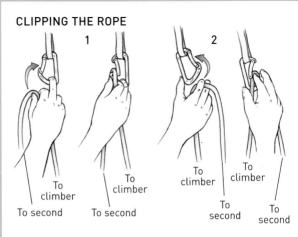

Fig. 26 Two methods of clipping the rope.
1 Hold the krab with the second or middle finger and clip the rope using thumb and index finger.
2 Hold the krab with the thumb and clip the rope with the index and second finger.

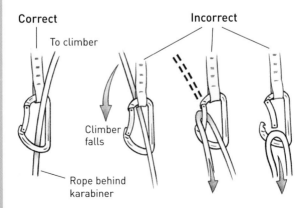

Fig. 27 Back clipping – the wrong way to clip a rope into a krab!

PLACING PROTECTION FOR TWO SECONDS

If you bring two seconds up a pitch, tied to the same rope, clip into runners as usual. When each second is tied into a separate rope, use the method below or request that the second, who is climbing first, clips the following climber's rope into vital pieces.

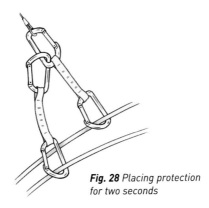

Fig. 28 *Placing protection for two seconds*

LOCKING OR OPEN GATE KRABS?

Use a screw gate krab when the consequence of the rope coming out of the krab is catastrophic, e.g. abseiling. Open gates are usually adequate on belay anchor placements, especially when using a clove hitch and you remain tight on your belay.

Screw gates are, however, advisable on all top and bottom rope belays because the movement of the system could cause the rope to come out of an open gate krab.

Avoid carrying a mixture of twist lock and screw gate krabs, because it is easy to forget to do up the screw gates.

DOUBLE ROPE TECHNIQUE (USING TWO HALF ROPES)

Advantages

- Each rope runs in a straighter line through the protection, an advantage that is lost if the ropes are crossed (Fig. 29).

- When a climber using a single rope pulls the rope to clip into a runner above their head, they momentarily increase the potential distance they could fall. Alternately clipping double ropes into protection reduces the length of a fall should you fail to clip the next piece of protection.

- They reduce the chances of complete rope failure.

- They reduce the amount of rope needed at belays.

- If the belayer is paying attention to both ropes, the IF is distributed between two runners and two ropes.

- On some traverses the leader can clip one rope into the runners then, as long as the belay is above the traverse, the other rope can protect the second along the traverse.

- Double ropes also give the option of a longer abseil.

Disadvantages

- Two ropes weigh more.

- Belaying a lead climber is more difficult as the belayer must take in and pay out ropes simultaneously.

Poor   Good

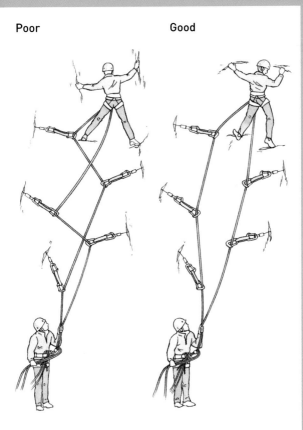

Fig. 29 *Poor and good double rope technique*

- **Solid anchors** Two are a minimum. Give each anchor a mark from one to five, where five is superb. Your belay should add up to ten, i.e. two superb anchors are enough.

- **Equalise the anchors** The belay should utilise all the anchors so that if part of it fails, the other anchors take the load with no movement of the belayer.

- **Independent anchors** Place anchors in separate sections of the cliff. Two nuts placed in the same crack are a single anchor point.

- **Tight rope** Keep the ropes taut – rope stretch may deposit the belayer over the edge.

- **Stand or sit?** Sit down when the anchors are below shoulder height to prevent you being pulled to your knees.

- **Communication** Easier when the second can be seen.

- **Direction of forces** Equalise the anchors so that a fall does not pull the belayer sideways or upwards.

- **What if?** Finally, ask 'what happens if the climber falls?' If the answer is anything other than 'nothing', look at the belay again.

ATTACHING THE ROPE TO ANCHORS

Figs 30 to 32 show a variety of simple methods.

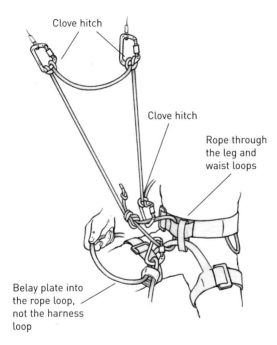

Clove hitch

Clove hitch

Rope through
the leg and
waist loops

Belay plate into
the rope loop,
not the harness
loop

Fig. 30 *Creating a belay when the anchors are within arm's
reach, or there is limited rope. The disadvantage of this
method is that it is difficult to adjust if you cannot reach the
anchors.*

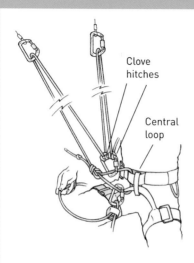

Clove hitches

Central loop

Fig. 31 *Creating a belay when the anchors are out of reach. Pass the rope through all the anchors. Take the loop/s of rope between the anchors and move to the edge. Attach a clove hitch to each rope and clip to the central loop with an HMS krab. All the adjustments are at the harness, but this method does use a lot of rope.*

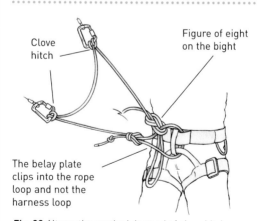

Clove hitch

Figure of eight on the bight

The belay plate clips into the rope loop and not the harness loop

Fig. 32 *Alternative method. Instead of clove hitches on an HMS krab, tie directly into the central loop with a figure of eight knot or two half hitches. Take a step towards the anchors before tying the knot.*

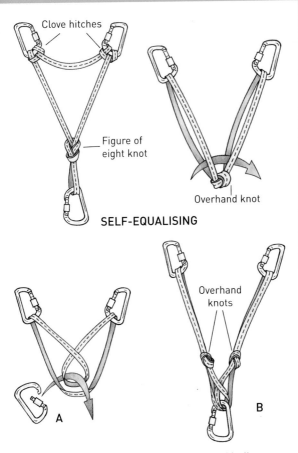

Clove hitches

Figure of
eight knot

Overhand knot

SELF-EQUALISING

Overhand
knots

A

B

Fig. 33 *Equalisation of anchors to a single point with slings to share the forces among the anchors, or to save rope when the anchors are far apart. Use 'self-equalising' when the anchors are strong and solid and when the belayer needs to move around a lot. The downside is that if one anchor fails, the other anchor is shock loaded. Placing knots in the sling can reduce this (B).*

The same principles apply when setting up an abseil station as they do for creating a normal belay: solid, independent and equalised anchors (Figs 34 and 35).

- Make the belay station high so that 'take off' and rope retrieval is easier.
- Easy angled routes provide more opportunities for the rope to snag.
- Avoid loose rock and use a rope protector on all sharp edges.
- Check that harnesses are buckled correctly.
- Tuck away hair, clothing and straps.

JOINING THE ROPES
The best method for joining ropes is an overhand knot (leaving 45cm of tail), pulled tight (Fig. 34). As it rolls over an edge it is less likely to become snagged. Do not use a figure of eight knot as it can invert. If you are nervous using a single overhand knot, tie two close together.

THROWING THE ROPE DOWN
Ensure that there is nobody beneath and check the ropes reach the bottom – only tie a knot in the rope end when you are unsure. To prevent double ropes becoming tangled tie different knots in each rope to mark the one to be pulled. Throw the ropes by layering across your hands (lap coiling) with decreasing sized layers. Grasp the middle and throw this down first. When it is windy, take the rope down loosely fed into a rucksack or create a large loop by tying an overhand knot and daisy chain the rope around the loop in a circle; this keeps the rope weighted throughout the throw.

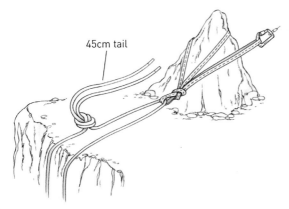

45cm tail

Fig. 34 *A retrievable abseil. Equalise the anchors with a separate short section of rope or slings. Put the abseil rope through the sling/s or clip into them using a krab. It is easier to pull the ropes down when they are exiting on the inside of the sling.*

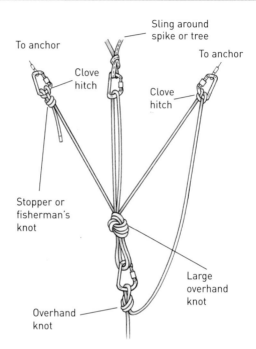

Fig. 35 *A fixed abseil station. Attach the rope using a clove hitch (for easy adjustment) to one anchor, then pass it through the other anchors and pull the rope between them to create V's. Tension the rope in the direction of the abseil and tie a figure of eight into the loops of rope. Clove hitch it to the final anchor. Tie a figure of eight or figure of nine in the rope to go over the cliff edge, and clip the remainder of rope into the figure of eight using a locking krab. If the full length of the rope is required, equalise the anchors with a separate length of rope slings.*

SLIDING DOWN THE ROPE

- Do not bounce; it can cut or abrade the rope.
- The ideal body position is 55 degrees to the cliff with feet apart, knees flexed and heels on the rock.
- To pass overhangs, flex the knees on the lip, push outwards and slide quickly down the rope. Alternatively, sit sideways and drop over the lip.
- The upper hand guides the rope and the bottom hand controls the rate of descent.
- When abseiling on a thin rope, increase friction by attaching the device to the rope using two HMS krabs or use Fig. 36. To remember which rope to pull and to remove twists, clip an extender from the harness to the rope to be pulled when you abseil.
- It is easier to abseil past a knot when the prusik is above the abseil device, and also more appropriate when using an Italian hitch.
- For all other situations, attach a French prusik from a leg loop to the rope below the abseil device (Fig. 37.1). Take care that the prusik does not reach the abseil device.
- To use two hands on the abseil rope, extend the abseil device away from the abseil loop with an extender and two screw gate krabs (Fig. 37.2). However, it puts the device closer to helmet straps, jacket toggles and hair, and it can make going over the edge more difficult.

The simplest method is for someone to hold the rope at the bottom of the abseil (not directly underneath in case of rock fall). If the abseiler lets go they can then pull the rope tightly, slowing their rate of descent.

Use the methods in Fig. 37 with caution and set them up so that the prusik cannot jam in the abseil device.

Fig. 36 Increasing the friction when using a thin rope

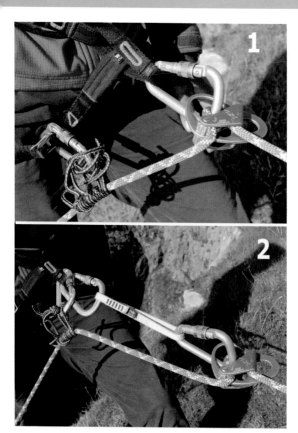

Fig. 37 Protecting an abseil with a prusik: *1* Prusik attached to leg loop, *2* Abseil device extended from the harness

If you have to stop mid-abseil and need both hands take the rope around your waist and wrap it around a leg (Fig. 38) or 'tie off' the abseil device.

Fig. 38

To retrieve an abseil rope:

- Check before the last person abseils that the ropes will come down and that they are not going to become jammed in a crack.
- If the rope is difficult to move, extend the abseil station.
- Separate and untangle the ropes before pulling. Remove knots and ensure you are pulling the correct one!
- Do not stand directly underneath the abseil.
- Pull ropes running through a sling slowly, otherwise 'glazing' damage can occur to the rope.
- If the rope remains stuck, try pulling at a different angle or pull heavily on both and then release the one you **do not** want to pull; the recoil of the unweighted rope may free it.
- Finally, get more people to pull. If the rope remains stuck and both ends of the rope are at the bottom, ascend on both ropes. If one end has disappeared part way up the rock, you can rope solo back to the anchors (Fig. 64, page 101).

THE CORDLETTE

This is a popular way to equalise multiple anchors using a very long rope cord. The cordlette does, however, create a large lump of cord on your harness and is largely unnecessary. Instead, equalise anchors using the rope whenever practical, because its dynamic properties help to absorb the forces created in a fall. Or use 120cm (48in) or 240cm (94in) equalised slings.

A multi-pitch route is simply a number of single pitches stacked on top of each other. Carry extra equipment, because some will be left at the belay. On remote routes carry a small bum bag with a first aid kit, some snacks, a small bivvy bag, a head torch and possibly shoes for the descent. Alternatively, carry a small first aid kit taped under your helmet.

In addition to the principles for creating a belay on a single-pitch climb you must also consider the forces that a leader falling on to the next pitch will create. The movement of the belayer upwards absorbs some of the force. However, it may be prudent to prevent an upward pull if there is a roof or rock spike above. Whether a direct or indirect belay (p. 23) is used depends on the difficulty of the climb, the terrain and whether you are swapping leads.

SINGLE-POINT ANCHOR

The most versatile way to attach to belay anchors is to equalise them to a single point using slings and attach your climbing rope to the slings via a clove hitch. This single anchor point can then be used to direct or semi-direct belay a second, making it easy to clip the second into the belay without having to swap ropes.

SWAPPING ROPES WHEN THE BELAY HAS BEEN SET UP USING ROPE

On reaching the belay stance, the lead climber attaches the rope to the anchors as in Fig. 30. If the second is not leading the next pitch, take their ropes underneath and through the middle of each anchor rope and into the anchor's krab. Alternatively clip another krab into the protection underneath the existing krabs. The leader's ropes will then be on top when leaving the stance.

HANGING STANCE

This stance is often required on a steep climb or at the base of a sea cliff. Do not struggle with one hand; clip into a good anchor and take tension on it while you create the belay. Equalise the anchors to a single point using slings. To belay the second, clip their rope through a belay anchor or a separate runner above you. To avoid twisting the rope, ensure that this krab is perpendicular to the rock.

STORING THE ROPES

A few seconds spent sorting the ropes will save time on the next pitch.

- Place the rope to cleanly feed to the belay device.
- Ensure the lead climber's ropes do not run over other ropes.
- Pull the ropes through so the leader's end is on top.
- On a hanging or restricted stance lay the climbing ropes across your anchor ropes, a rock spike or slings with progressively shorter loops. Attach loops of rope to an HMS krab using a slippery hitch (Fig. 4.16).
- When abseiling into a small or a hanging stance, e.g. just above the sea, store the climbing rope in a light rope bag or a rucksack. Ensure that both lead ends are at the top of the pile.

PREVENTING FALL FACTOR 2

Place a runner as soon as you leave the belay. If you cannot find a runner, clip an extender into the belay, but remember that the force on that runner is almost doubled.

- When the way down is not obvious, lower someone down to check the route – if it is incorrect, belay them back up.
- Be organised and have a method for rapidly attaching yourself and your partner to each belay. Tie a lark's foot sling to the abseil loop on your harness and tie several knots to create loops for attachment at different points along its length (cow's tail). Then attach your abseil device to the first loop on the cow's tail or into your harness abseil loop.
- The first person abseils, protected by a prusik.
- When the belay is reached, they attach to it via the cow's tail, and then remove the belay device and tie the ends into the belay. Finally, they should protect the second by holding on to the ropes.
- When the second has arrived, pull the ropes feeding the one being pulled down through the belay, ready for the next abseil.
- If it is windy take the ropes down, loosely fed into a rucksack that is hung from the abseil device.

EMERGENCY DEVICES FOR ABSEILING
- If you only have one device between two, pull the belay device back up after the first has abseiled or create a karabiner brake (Fig. 39).
- Always use two opposing open gate krabs to create the platform (the collars on locking krabs get in the way) and attach the krabs to your harness with a locking krab.
- You can use an Italian hitch, but it twists the rope. If you have to use it with double ropes, put the Italian hitches on separate krabs and extend one away from the other. The person with the abseil device should go last to remove the kinks.

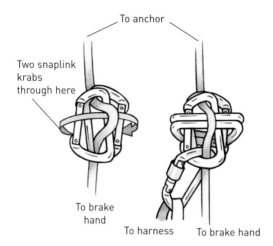

Fig. 39 Using krabs to create a karabiner brake

- If this does not create enough friction, set up another karabiner brake and link the two together using a wired nut. Ensure that the rope passes over the back bar of the krab, and not the gate.

ABSEILING WITH DIFFERENT DIAMETER ROPES
Some long routes are climbed using a single rope with the second dragging a 7–9mm rope for abseiling. The thinner rope stretches more and travels through the abseil device faster. To avoid a disaster, ensure the thicker rope is through the abseil anchor and that the bottom ends of the rope are tied together. Alternatively, use the method in Fig. 40.

ABSEILING ON A DAMAGED ROPE

When one rope has been damaged, abseil on the good rope and use the other one to pull the ropes down (Fig. 40). Take great care pulling the ropes down, because should they become jammed, you will have to use the damaged rope or the thin line to climb back up the cliff.

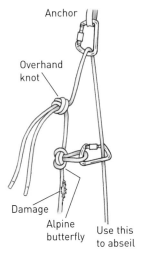

Anchor

Overhand knot

Damage

Alpine butterfly   *Use this to abseil*

***Fig. 40** Abseiling on a damaged or thinner rope*

ABSEILING PAST A KNOT

Occasionally two ropes are joined for accessing a big sea cliff, or to escape from a route (Fig. 41). To pass the knot it is essential that the French prusik is on an extender above the abseil device (but within reach).

- When you are close to the knot, stop, load the French prusik, remove the belay tube and replace it below the knot (Fig. 41A and 41B).

- Release the French prusik so that your weight comes on to the belay device (take care that the prusik does not come up against the knot – Fig. 41B).

- If you cannot release the French prusik, stand in another prusik placed between the abseil device and release the stuck one.

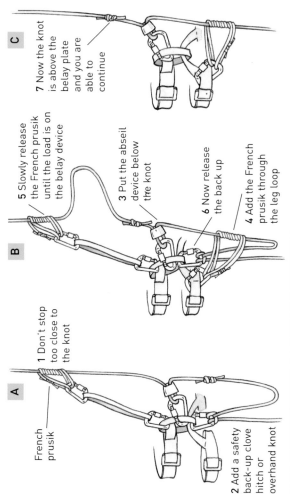

C

7 Now the knot is above the belay plate and you are able to continue

B

5 Slowly release the French prusik until the load is on the belay device

3 Put the abseil device below the knot

6 Now release the back up

4 Add the French prusik through the leg loop

A

1 Don't stop too close to the knot

French prusik

2 Add a safety back-up clove hitch or overhand knot

Fig. 41 *Abseiling past a knot: follow steps 1–7 to complete the procedure.*

Sport climbs are the ultimate convenience climbs – all you need to climb are a single rope, a belay device, 12–15 quick draws and a single 60m rope. Sport climbing is simpler, but that can lead to complacency.

- When practising falling, double-up protection and fall at the top of a climb to reduce the wear and tear on your rope (use more rope to absorb the force).
- A calm, supple body is less susceptible to injury, so fall gracefully, in control, facing the rock, and try to avoid tumbling.
- If you fall on a slab, slide down on your feet, gently pushing away with your hands.
- Keep legs bent and apart to act as shock absorbers.
- Keep the rope running cleanly; a rope wrapped around a leg can tip you upside down.
- Be careful when grabbing the rope as you fly past; it can result in rope burns.

GETTING BACK TO THE ROCK
- When the leader can reach the rope running to the belayer, pull down on it and pulley yourself back to your high point. The belayer should be taking in the slack rope.
- When the leader is hanging in space, use a strenuous technique called 'snapping'. It requires good teamwork – the leader pulls up on their rope and lets go; the belayer simultaneously takes in. The belayer should sit on the rope, then as the climber releases the rope the belayer sits further down, takes in as he stands and continues to repeat the process.

Most sports routes have a 'lower off' at the top, consisting of two bolts and possibly a linking chain or sling. **Note: If the lower off is a sling do not – under any circumstances – lower from the sling itself, but use a krab.**

● Before climbing, ensure that there is enough rope to lower back down, tie a knot in the end or tie into the spare end. If you have started to lower and there is not enough rope, tie another rope to it and bypass the knot using a second belay device (this is easier with a third person to help).

There are two methods, A and B, shown in Fig. 42. When you need maximum length of rope, use B, as described here:

● Take several metres of slack and attach it to your harness using a clove hitch.

● Untie from the end of the rope and thread it through a lower-off point.

● Re-tie into the end and detach the rope from your harness.

● Before lowering take the tension on the rope, checking everything is correct and your belayer is awake, then remove the quick draws or sling and lower.

● Alternatively, tie another rope to it and bypass the knot using a second belay device (still on the original belayer's harness).

When the climb is so steep that you cannot easily retrieve the quick draws, clip one from your harness to the climbing rope to keep closer to the cliff. Be careful removing the last clip, because you could take your belayer with you as you swing out.

A

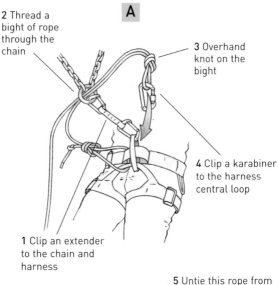

2 Thread a bight of rope through the chain

3 Overhand knot on the bight

4 Clip a karabiner to the harness central loop

1 Clip an extender to the chain and harness

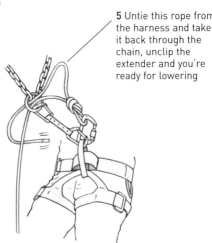

5 Untie this rope from the harness and take it back through the chain, unclip the extender and you're ready for lowering

SPORT CLIMBING

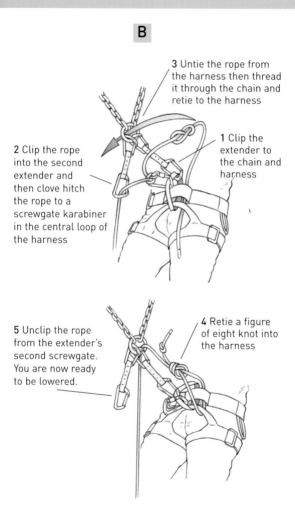

B

3 Untie the rope from the harness then thread it through the chain and retie to the harness

1 Clip the extender to the chain and harness

2 Clip the rope into the second extender and then clove hitch the rope to a screwgate karabiner in the central loop of the harness

5 Unclip the rope from the extender's second screwgate. You are now ready to be lowered.

4 Retie a figure of eight knot into the harness

***Fig. 42** Two methods (A and B) for lowering from a sports climb (the numbers 1–5 show the correct sequence)*

The same factors regarding belays apply to the setting up of a bottom rope, as for any belay. Avoid using cams, because the weighting and un-weighting of the rope may cause them to walk deeper into cracks.

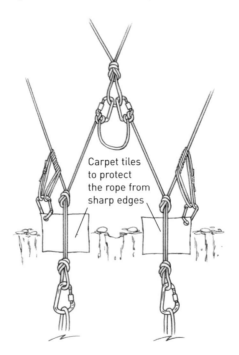

Carpet tiles to protect the rope from sharp edges

Fig. 43 *A hitching rail creates a flexible attachment system. A pre-stretched rope reduces wear and tear on edges. Clove hitches on the central anchors provide independent adjustments of the ropes. The attachment rope for the climbing rope must be over the edge and should be two locking krabs, with their gates pointing downwards (vibrations can undo the gates) and in the same direction.*

IMPROVISED CHEST HARNESSES

You can create an improvised chest harness using a sling (see below).

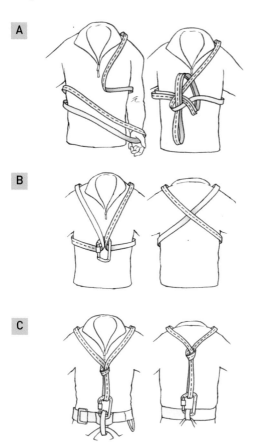

Fig. 44 *(A) Parisian baudrier, (B) cross system and (C) improved method*

COILING ROPES

Lap coiling (Fig 41a) and daisy chaining (Fig 41b) reduces kinks. The old-fashioned 'mountaineer's coil' introduces kinks into the rope, but when divided between two people it can be used to carry an injured person.

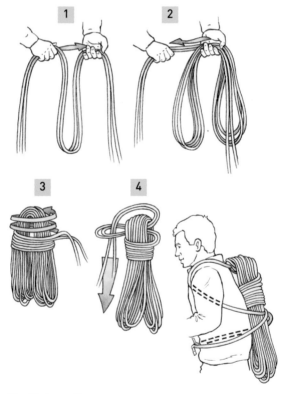

Fig. 45a *Lap coiling*

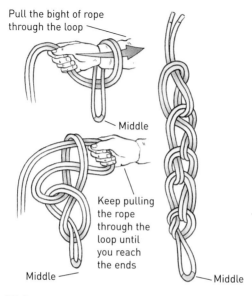

Pull the bight of rope through the loop

Middle

Keep pulling the rope through the loop until you reach the ends

Middle

Middle

Fig. 45b *Daisy chaining*

EXPERT TIP

Louise Thomas, BMG/IFMGA Mountain Guide
[Twid turner@aol.com
www.sheersummits.com

'The rope is no use in the bottom of your rucksack. It is best carried uncoiled in a stuff sac, with the end protruding out of the lid for easy access.'

Rescue techniques are seldom used and regular practice is important – they are not a fire drill. For simplicity, all rescues are described using a single rope (although double ropes can make it easier they stretch more and prusiks do not grip as well). Carry a knife, even if it is only used to cut abseil tat into short lengths.

- Everyone should know what to do if they lose contact with the rock.
- Choose stances that allow communication.
- Extend runners to reduce friction.
- Pitches that end with loose rock put the second at greater risk.
- Maintain the condition of your climbing and rescue equipment.
- Keep the rope/s tidy.
- Create a simple belay and belay diligently.
- Remove all jewellery.
- Have first aid training.

WARNING

A loaded rope is cut very easily; when practising, consider using a separate rope to protect the victim.

!

PRUSIK CORD

- 1.3m of 5 or 6mm soft kernmantle cord tied with a double fisherman's knot is best.
- The ideal number of prusik loops is three.
- Shorter prusiks maintain the tension on the rope better than long ones. Elongate them with a sling if necessary.

AT THE BELAY

Ensure that you arrive at belays with enough equipment to carry out a rescue – two or three Prusiks, a long sling, a few krabs and extenders should be enough. Belay anchors equalised to a single point make life simpler.

Alternatively, take the second's rope through a high krab when you think they may fall off, allowing a pulley system to be set up easily. However, this does make an assisted hoist more difficult as the fallen climber will only be on one runner.

Fig. 46 The Mariner hitch – a useful hitch for lowering someone past a knot when two ropes have been tied together. It can come undone if the tension is removed.

- Tie off the belay plate.
- Take a deep breath, stay calm and think carefully.
- Look, listen and shout for help.
- Ask 'what happens if?' at every stage of the rescue:
  - Can you rescue the victim while still attached to the belay? Is the injured climber conscious? Do you need to give first aid? Is it quicker to go for help? Are there any climbers on an adjacent route?
  - It is always quicker and easier to descend rather than ascend with a victim.

RESCUE TOOLS
Mechanical devices
Mechanical devices must be pushed forward to release them, therefore ensure you do not push any ascender hard up against a knot.

Prusik knots
Releasing under load (autoblocs) (Fig. 47) The French prusik is essential for many rescues, but use with care, because it can release very easily and can be untied when loaded.

Fig. 47 French prusik (marchard knot). To release it when loaded, push firmly on the end of the hitch furthest from the krab (do not pull the whole pitch).

Gripping the rope (Fig. 48) The Klemheist is used when failure to grip the rope is disastrous. It is not easily released when a climber's weight is on it and may remain jammed when the climber is removed.

Fig. 48 *The Klemheist. More turns increase the grip (tie it using cord or tape).*

DESCENDING AND ASCENDING THE ROPE
Your strength, agility and arm length dictate the distance between the prusik, or ascender, and your harness. To prevent a catastrophe, attach the rope into your harness at frequent intervals using a clove hitch or a figure of eight via a screw gate krab. See Figs 49–51.

ABSEILING AND RE-ASCENDING
If you have to descend to an injured climber and re-ascend to the belay, it is best to abseil with a Klemheist attached above the abseil device. When you want to ascend remove the abseil device and attach a French prusik or garda hitch for the foot to ascend (Fig. 51).

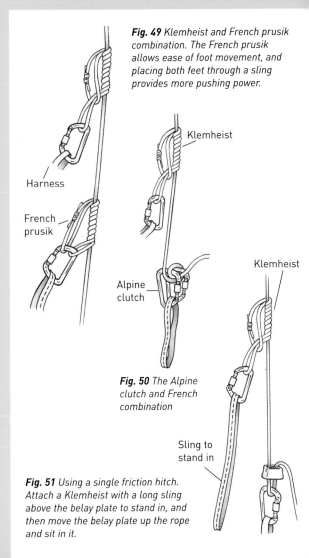

Fig. 49 Klemheist and French prusik combination. The French prusik allows ease of foot movement, and placing both feet through a sling provides more pushing power.

Klemheist

Harness

French prusik

Alpine clutch

Fig. 50 The Alpine clutch and French combination

Klemheist

Sling to stand in

Fig. 51 Using a single friction hitch. Attach a Klemheist with a long sling above the belay plate to stand in, and then move the belay plate up the rope and sit in it.

Hoisting is hard on your back so use a pulley system. If the second cannot unclip from the runners as they are hoisted, you will have to abseil and remove them.

RESCUES WITHOUT LEAVING THE BELAY
Figs 52–54 examine rescues where you do not leave the belay.

The in-situ assisted hoist (Fig. 52)
The climber in difficulty can assist by pulling on a loop of their climbing rope. This system is limited by several factors:

- Does the loop of rope reach the fallen climber?
- Are they within sight?
- Can the victim hear and carry out instructions?

ALPINE CLUTCH (Fig. 50)

When used as part of a pulley system, the alpine clutch generates friction reducing overall efficiency. It is mainly used when there is a shortage of prusik loops. It is difficult to release and lower a climber, but clipping the rope inbetween the original krabs and pulling downwards can free it.

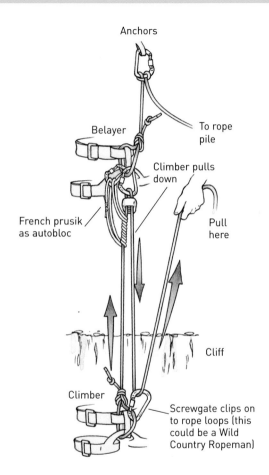

Anchors

To rope pile

Belayer

Climber pulls down

French prusik as autobloc

Pull here

Cliff

Climber

Screwgate clips on to rope loops (this could be a Wild Country Ropeman)

Fig. 52 *The in-situ assisted hoist – a strenuous method on steep rock. Push the French prusik forward if a rest is required.*

The in-situ counterbalance hoist [Fig. 53]

- **Advantages** Works well on restricted stances and is faster than any other method. If you must go to the victim, it is simple to change to a counterbalance abseil.
- **Disadvantage** Only easily accomplished when the anchors are brought to a single point with a sling.

Step 1 Tie off the belay device.

Step 2 Attach a French prusik from the live rope to the anchors [if this cannot be done, attach a Klemheist to all the anchor ropes and link the French to this]. Then transfer the load from the belay plate to the prusik.

Step 3 Put a screw gate krab on the anchor.

Step 4 Pull a bight of rope from between the prusik and belay plate [leave the plate in place] and clip it into the screw gate. You are now in a counterbalance.

Step 5 Lengthen your tie-in point to the anchor to give yourself enough room to move. Work yourself up the rope towards the anchors, lean back and pull up on the live rope – if the climber decides to help, you may shoot backwards!

When the bottom Klemheist reaches the belay device push it down the rope. To avoid loosing precious height gained, push the French prusik down before taking the load.

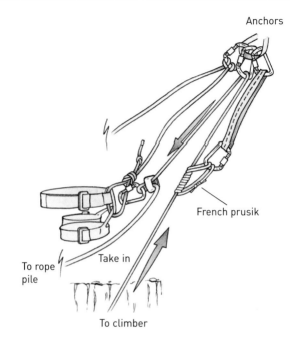

Anchors

French prusik

To rope pile

Take in

To climber

Fig. 53 The in-situ counterbalance hoist

The 'in-situ' unassisted hoist ('Z' pulley, Fig. 54)

The in-situ unassisted hoist is used when the fallen climber cannot assist you. It is only useful when the hoist is a short distance. This pulley has a 3:1 advantage i.e. for every 3m pulled the victim gains 1m.

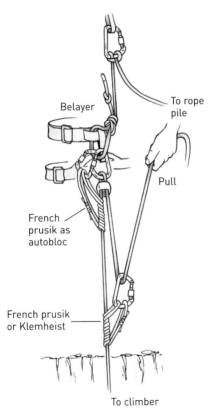

Belayer

To rope pile

Pull

French prusik as autobloc

French prusik or Klemheist

To climber

Fig. 54 The in-situ unassisted hoist

In-situ rescue of a climber on a traverse (Fig. 55)

Step 1 Tie off the belay plate and attach a French prusik from the belay or central loop to the loaded rope.

Step 2 Throw a loop of rope or the end of the rope, if available, to the victim to clip into the belay loop of their harness. This rope is then attached to an Italian hitch on the anchors.

Step 3 With or without the help of the victim, lower the loaded rope and pull the victim below the belay.

Step 4 The victim may be able to climb to the belay. If the climber is free, it is necessary to create a hoist.

Step 5 Retrieve the runners from the traverse. The easiest way is to be belayed back along the traverse and back to the belay.

Steps 1, 2 & 3

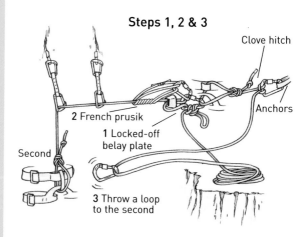

Fig. 55 Follow the numbers 1–9 in order to complete the procedure (continued on page 83)

Steps 4, 5 & 6

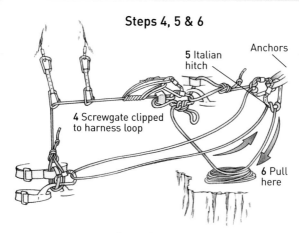

Anchors

5 Italian hitch

4 Screwgate clipped to harness loop

6 Pull here

Steps 7, 8 & 9

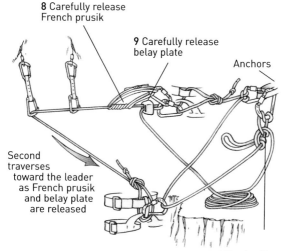

8 Carefully release French prusik

9 Carefully release belay plate

Anchors

Second traverses toward the leader as French prusik and belay plate are released

7 Lock-off Italian hitch

If you need to escape from the belay, your first option is to remove your harness. If you need your harness use one of the following methods. When you cannot reach the anchors, consider tying an alpine butterfly close to your central loop and use that as the belay loop (Fig. 56).

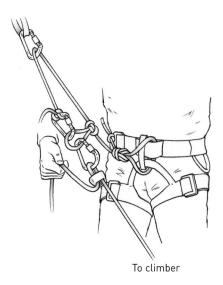

To climber

Fig. 56 *Tying into an alpine butterfly can make rescues and escape from the belay very simple.*

WHEN BELAY ANCHORS ARE WITHIN REACH
(Fig. 57)

If the belay is set up using the climbing rope:

Step 1 Tie off the belay plate device.

Step 2 Create a single-point belay using slings (if not already in place).

Step 3 Place a French prusik in front of the belay device and attach it to the new sling belay. If only one solid anchor can be reached, use it, but improve it as soon possible. If it is suspect, follow the procedure as though you cannot reach the belay.

Step 4 Release the live rope slowly on to the French prusik. Remove the belay device and retie the rope into the sling using a tied-off Italian hitch.

If you are using a direct belaying method:

Step 1 Tie off the belay plate.

Step 2 Place a cow's tail on the harness and clip into the belay.

Step 3 Untie from the rope and release it from the belay.

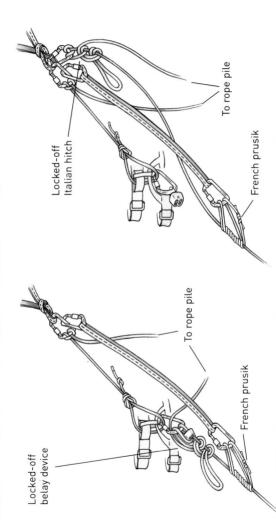

Locked-off
Italian hitch

To rope pile

French prusik

Locked-off
belay device

To rope pile

French prusik

Fig. 57 When the belay anchors are within reach and set up using slings equalised to a single point.

WHEN BELAY ANCHORS ARE OUT OF REACH
(Fig. 58)

Step 1 Tie off the belay plate and attach a French prusik from the live rope to a Klemheist on the anchor ropes created with a 240cm sling with as many turns around the rope as possible.

Step 2 Lower the load on to the French prusik. Remove the belay plate and untie from the rope (protect yourself with a sling if necessary). Leave any knots tied in the end of the rope in place.

There are now two options depending on whether you need all the rope to effect a rescue.

OPTION 1 p. 89: When you need the full length of the rope

Step 4 Set up another belay from the same anchors using slings.

Step 5 Attach the live rope to the sling belay with a tied-off Italian hitch.

Step 6 Release the French prusik and lower the live rope onto the tied-off Italian hitch.

Step 7 Remove the rope creating the belay.

OPTION 2 p. 89: When you do not need the full length of the rope

Step 4 Tie a knot in the anchor ropes below the Klemheist and attach the live rope to the knot with a tied-off Italian hitch. If you cannot tie all the ropes together, tie a knot in the rope you were attached to and attach the live ropes to the Klemheist.

Step 5 Release the French prusik and lower the live rope on to the tied-off Italian hitch.

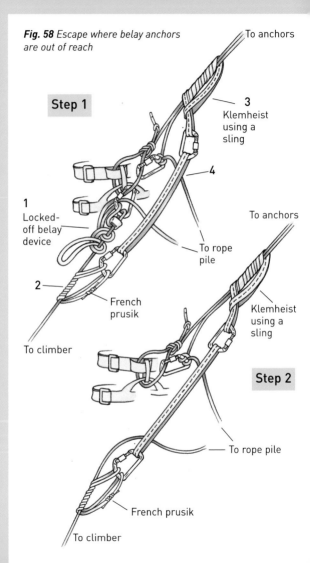

Fig. 58 Escape where belay anchors are out of reach

To anchors

Step 1

3
Klemheist using a sling

4

1
Locked-off belay device

2

French prusik

To rope pile

To climber

To anchors

Klemheist using a sling

Step 2

To rope pile

French prusik

To climber

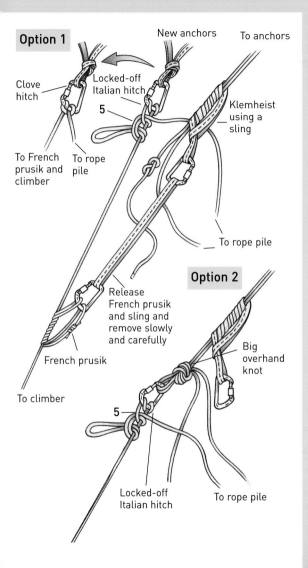

Option 1

New anchors

To anchors

Clove hitch

Locked-off Italian hitch

5

Klemheist using a sling

To French prusik and climber

To rope pile

To rope pile

Release French prusik and sling and remove slowly and carefully

Option 2

Big overhand knot

French prusik

To climber

5

Locked-off Italian hitch

To rope pile

What you do after escape from the belay will depend on how the belay is set up, how injured the climber is and how close to the top you are. The following options are available:

1 LOWER THE INJURED CLIMBER

If the ground is less than 50m away, lower the victim to the ground. The rescuer can abseil and retrieve the rope later. Two ropes allow a longer lower, but require you to pass a knot during the lower (Fig. 59).

Step 1 When the knot comes 1m away from the belay device, attach a French prusik in front of the device and link it to the belay via a tied-off Italian hitch.

Step 2 Lower the weight on to the French prusik and tie off the spare rope to the belay.

Step 3 Remove the belay device and replace it behind the knot, then release the French prusik.

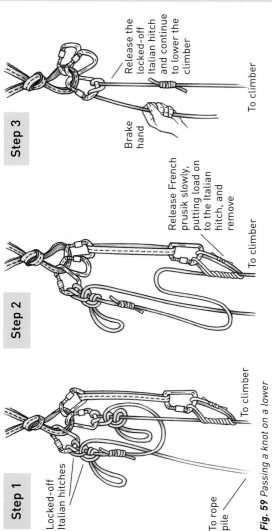

Step 1

Locked-off Italian hitches

To rope pile

To climber

Step 2

Release French prusik slowly, putting load on to the Italian hitch, and remove

To climber

Step 3

Release the locked-off Italian hitch and continue to lower the climber

Brake hand

To climber

Fig. 59 Passing a knot on a lower

2 LOWER/COUNTERBALANCE ABSEIL (Fig. 60)
Counterbalance systems are complex and require strong anchors, the equipment must be left behind and they involve a moving rope through a krab. Revert to simpler systems as soon as possible.

Step 1 Lower the injured climber almost half a rope-length (or one rope-length if two ropes are available) to an intermediate ledge from which to make an escape.

Step 2 Place a French prusik on to the live rope (A).

Step 3 Remove the Italian hitch and replace the rope through the krab. Attach the abseil device from the instructor's harness to the dead rope. The instructor's weight counterbalances the climber (B).

Step 4 Transfer the French prusik from the live rope to protect the abseil (B).

If there is a big weight difference between the climbers, leave an Italian hitch in place. Remember to tie a knot in the end of the abseil rope.

3 RESCUING AN INJURED CLIMBER ON A TRAVERSE
Belays at the end of traverses are not usually good at directing the forces to the belay. Add anchors to better direct the forces.

Step 1 Escape the belay and protect yourself across the traverse, preferably with a mechanical ascender or two cow's tails.

Step 2 Set up a new belay.

Step 3 Transfer the loaded rope to the belay.

Step 4 Once you are above the victim, set up a new belay, transfer them to it, return to your belay, dismantle it and rope solo to the new belay. Then hoist or descend.

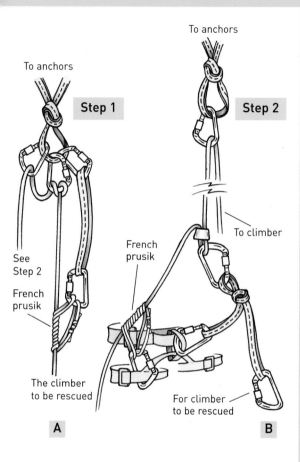

Fig. 60 *Lower/counterbalance abseil (**note**: ensure that you can reach the climber!)*

When descending is not an option, hoist the injured climber on to the belay stance (remember runners must be removed before an injured climber can be hoisted). Once out of the system it is much easier to create an efficient pulley. The actual hoist is the same as Fig. 53, p. 80.

Step 1 Place a French prusik in front of the tied-off Italian hitch and attach it to a krab in the belay.

Step 2 Take some rope and put it through another krab. Remove the Italian hitch and put a Klemheist in front of the French prusik.

Step 3 Attach the dead rope to the Klemheist via two krabs or, even better, a pulley to reduce friction. Pull. If the climber is difficult to hoist, try attaching the rope to your harness with an Italian hitch and use your leg muscles to pull.

Improving the efficiency of the hoist (Fig. 61)
There are ways of increasing the efficiency of a pulley, but increasing it beyond 6:1 is not worth consideration, due to the friction.

Assisted abseil
Once the injured climber has either been lowered or hoisted on to the belay stance you may want to abseil with them (Fig. 60B shows the set-up for the belay device).

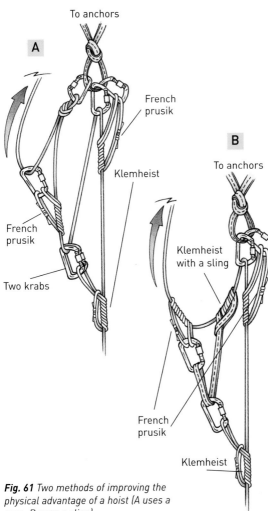

To anchors

A

French prusik

Klemheist

French prusik

Two krabs

B

To anchors

Klemheist with a sling

French prusik

Klemheist

Fig. 61 *Two methods of improving the physical advantage of a hoist (A uses a rope, B uses a sling).*

Removing the weight from a rope to untie the victim

The climber may be dangling on the rope and need to be transferred to a new belay. Attach them to the belay and use Fig. 62 to untie the knot.

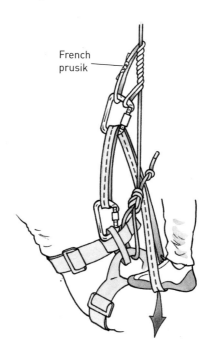

French prusik

Fig. 62 *Removing the weight*

Before attempting to rescue a lead climber who cannot be lowered the security of the top anchor must be beyond question. See Fig. 63 over.

Step 1 Create a solid ground anchor and attach to it using an Italian hitch.

Step 2 Escape the belay.

Step 3 Ascend to the injured climber. Because the rope is tensioned, it is not possible to use back-up knots. Therefore use two Klemheists attached to your waist. Unclip any anchors, but do not remove them; clip them into the rope below you.

Step 4 Reinforce the top anchor or create a new anchor.

Step 5 Clip the injured climber to the new anchors using a mariner knot or a tied-off Italian hitch. If necessary, attach a chest harness to the climber.

Step 6 Connect the rope you have ascended to the anchors.

Step 7 Descend and remove the bottom anchors.

Step 8 Ascend back to the anchors, removing any gear on the way.

You now have a number of options:

OPTION 1 Lower the climber to the ground.

OPTION 2 Solo climb out and get help or hoist the climber.

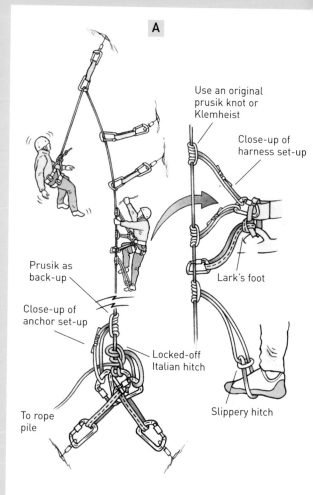

A

Use an original
prusik knot or
Klemheist

Close-up of
harness set-up

Prusik as
back-up

Lark's foot

Close-up of
anchor set-up

Locked-off
Italian hitch

To rope
pile

Slippery hitch

Fig. 63 Rescuing an injured lead climber: (A) Ascend to a
stricken climber, (B) Create a new belay

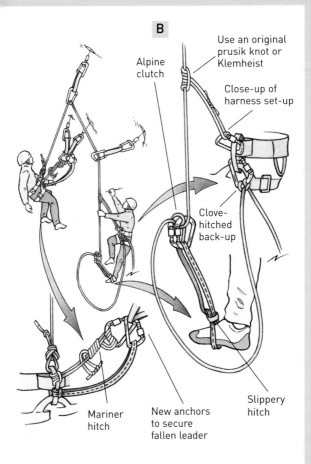

B

Use an original prusik knot or Klemheist

Alpine clutch

Close-up of harness set-up

Clove-hitched back-up

Mariner hitch

New anchors to secure fallen leader

Slippery hitch

If the accident has occurred close to the top of the crag, rope soloing is the safest method to get out, but you require enough rope to reach the top of the crag. The same system is used whether aid climbing or free climbing (Fig. 64).

Step 1 Set up an upward pulling anchor and tie the rope into it with a double figure of eight or figure of nine knot.

Step 2 Tie into the other end of the rope.

Step 3 From the anchor, take 4m of rope, tie a figure of eight knot and clip it into your harness with a screw gate krab.

Step 4 Take 2m of rope from the upward pulling anchor and tie a clove hitch.

Step 5 As you climb clip the rope below your clove hitch into the placements.

Step 6 When you reach the clove hitch, readjust it to pay out the amount of slack you are comfortable with.

Step 7 When the clove hitch meets the figure of eight take a new 4m and attach it to your harness then undo the original figure of eight. Continue climbing as before.

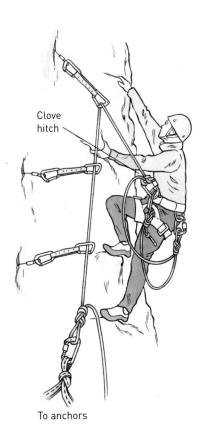

Clove
hitch

To anchors

Fig. 64 *Solo climbing*

Aid climbing is simply pulling on gear rather than the rock. Because of the likelihood of placements coming out, you may wear safety glasses. For big walling tactics and techniques see *Mountaineering* (A&C Black, 2008).

AIDING EQUIPMENT

Bandolier or chest rack – Bandoliers get in the way; buy a chest racking system.

Cheater stick – Used for placing out-of-reach gear.

Daisy chains – Connect each etrier to your harness, connect you to a belay and for many other jobs.

Etriers/aiders – Four- or five-rung webbing ladders.

Fifi hooks – Sometimes attached to the top of each etrier, via a short sling, to enable easy retrieval of the etrier from below. However, they can unclip – notchless open-gate krabs are recommended for novices.

Footwear – Choose a shoe with a stiffish, sticky midsole and a protective rand.

Harness – With plenty of gear loops and a haul loop on the rear.

Helmet – Wear one!

Krabs – Any will do, but oval krabs don't shift on equipment when loaded.

Mechanical (handled) ascenders – Essential for serious ascending.

Pegs – There are two types: blades and angles.

Peg hammers – A flat hammer for placing pegs and a blunt pick for removing them.

Protection – A wider variety of nuts and camming devices than normal is required.

Ropes – A good condition 50–60m/11mm rope is best with a spare 11mm dynamic rope towed as a haul line.

Sky hooks – Hard, steel hooks in a variety of shapes to grip ledges and holes.

Slings – They save carrying extra krabs and are used for tying off pegs and extending the rope over roofs.

Zip line – A 7–9mm rope for hauling equipment, water or food in the middle of an aid pitch.

Aid equipment is not dissimilar to that found on any climber's rack, with some additions and a lot more of it! Less gear can be carried if you reach as high as possible and remove pieces from below (back cleaning).

PLACING PEGS (p. 34)

There are some peculiarities that must be mastered for aid climbing:

- Excessive hammering wastes energy; balance how well pegs are embedded against how difficult it is to remove them.
- Stacked pegs are easily lost. Clip them together with a sling before hammering.
- Stack blades back to back.
- Avoid stacking angles one on top of another (unless the inside one is much smaller). Stack angles facing each other.
- Z pitons are very useful for stacking.
- Pegs can be placed alongside a nut. Clip the wedge to the peg. Whether you weight the peg or the wedge depends on the placement.

USING SKY HOOKS

- Keep them to the rear of your harness and don't carry them on one krab (they are easily dropped).
- Start from a solid runner and clip a krab full of hooks to each aider.
- Do not bounce-test hooks.
- Keep your weight on the lower hook as you transfer to the new one, otherwise it may pop off.
- If you are leaving sky hooks behind, tape them down to stay in place.
- Avoid hammering sky hooks into bolt holes, because it increases the chance of them coming out and damages the hole for future placements.

Approach an aid climb as you would a free climb: rack up precisely, plan ahead for good placements and rests, reduce rope drag etc.

- Keep three or four pitons per krab on one side and standard gear on the other.
- Keep your hammer and ascenders accessible at all times.
- Aid climbing overhangs creates difficulties, but a daisy chain enables you to hang from your harness in a stable position. A chest harness may be useful when the overhang approaches horizontal.

There are many variations on a theme, but here is one basic system (Fig. 65).

Step 1 Place an aid piece at the furthest point you can reach.

Step 2 Clip in two krabs separately (the second takes the climbing rope). If you have placed a peg, put a small sling on to it and then clip the two krabs into the sling. Do not clip the climbing rope into the piece unless the placement you are standing on is poor and the higher piece is more solid.

Step 3 Clip an etrier to the krab without the rope. Test the piece with a gentle one-footed hop or, if it is poor, ease from one etrier to the other slowly. If it is very steep you can clip yourself into the daisy chain via the fifi hook.

Step 4 Remove your second etrier from the lower piece and clip it into the same krab.

Step 5 Move on to the etriers fully and clip your fifi hook into the new piece or to your daisy chain.

Step 6 Clip into the climbing rope.

Step 7 Stand as high as you can and repeat.

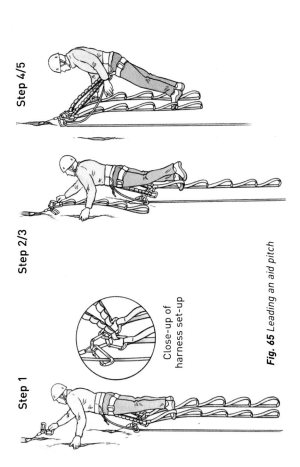

Step 4/5

Step 2/3

Close-up of
harness set-up

Step 1

Fig. 65 *Leading an aid pitch*

HIGH STEPPING (Fig. 66)

You may need to step on to an etrier to reach as far as you can. It is unnerving, but made easier if there are hand holds or the rock is easy-angled. Maintain body tension at all times on steep/overhanging rock. The daisy chain can take the strain on your body, but the resulting upward pull increases the chance of the lower aid piece coming out, especially if it is a sky hook.

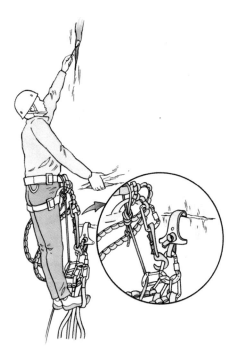

Fig. 66 High stepping

RESTING
Tuck a leg under your rear (your bottom on your bent leg). Don't ask the belayer to take the rope tight because it simply increases the forces on the placement.

TESTING DUBIOUS PLACEMENTS
Ease on to it Ease your weight off the present piece and on to the next piece, hoping it will hold full body weight.

Shock-test Bounce on the next piece (with the aiders and daisy clipped in), slowly at first, gradually building up to forces exceeding body weight. The skill is in preventing the present piece from getting shock-loaded if the tested piece does pull. Testing in the middle of a string of marginal placements is one of the scariest parts of aid climbing. **Note:** Do not shock-test sky hooks.

Funkness device This is a short length of cable that is clipped to the piece and jerked with a hammer clipped to the other end. They generate amazing amounts of force and may ruin a piece – use them carefully.

CREATING A BELAY STANCE
This requires a lot of thought, especially when sac hauling on a big wall. It is best to create separate single point belays for the ascending rope and the hauling rope.

TENSION TRAVERSES AND PENDULUMS

When the gap between cracks is small, the lead climber simply uses tension from the rope to reach another crack or hold. When the gap is greater, the leader must place a solid runner as high as possible. From this they are lowered down just enough to run across the cliff to the next crack. Longer pendulums can be abseiled with the leader still belayed on the climbing rope. Then abseil rope is left for the second (but you require an extra rope).

Once the new crack has been gained the higher you can climb before clipping the climbing rope into protection, the easier and safer it is for the second to follow.

The difficult part of a pendulum falls to the second. If it is a short pendulum, you may be able to simply unclip and swing across. When it is longer, lower your-self across until the lead rope can take your weight (Fig. 67). Clip into the pendulum point using a daisy chain. For a short pendulum, pass a bight of rope through the protection you are lowering from and either clip it into your harness or hold on tightly. Take as much slack rope as you can until it is tight. Attach your ascender to the rope you want to eventually ascend and lower yourself across. Once your weight is on the lead rope you can retrieve the double strand and continue up the pitch.

If there is not enough rope, untie and put a single strand of rope through the krab you are leaving behind. If the pendulum is very large an extra rope will make life easier for the second.

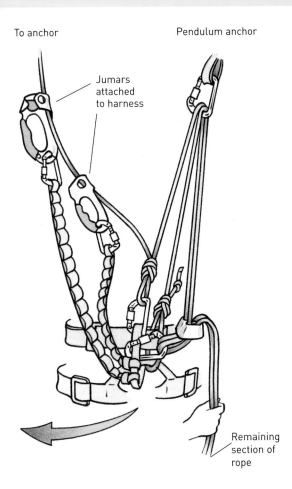

To anchor

Pendulum anchor

Jumars
attached
to harness

Remaining
section of
rope

Fig. 67 *Seconding a pendulum*

AID CLIMBING

If the pitch is very short, aid to remove the placements. Follow the same sequence as the leader (but remove the climbing rope before stepping on to the etriers).

For longer pitches, ascend the rope using one of the following methods, which are faster.

CLEANING AN AID PITCH (METHOD ONE)

See Fig. 68. The free end of the daisy chain is linked to an etrier. The separate connection allows you to clip into a piece of protection or anchor without taking the ascender off the rope. Particularly useful when cleaning traverses.

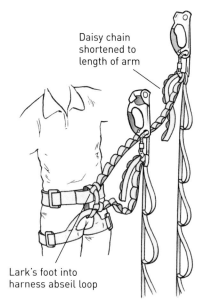

Daisy chain shortened to length of arm

Lark's foot into harness abseil loop

Fig. 68 Method one. Ensure the top ascender can be reached by a full arm extension. The lower daisy chain is shorter and the top ascender should be the dominant hold.

CLEANING AN AID PITCH (METHOD TWO)

A Petzl Croll ascender is attached to a chest harness using a semi-circular Maillon and a smaller oval Maillon.

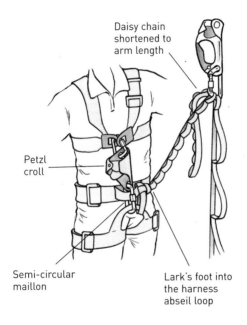

Daisy chain shortened to arm length

Petzl croll

Semi-circular maillon

Lark's foot into the harness abseil loop

Fig. 69 Method two

CLEANING AN AID PITCH (METHOD THREE)

Set up the ascenders for your arm length with slings, and not etriers.

- Keep your movements smooth and let your legs do the work.
- Attach a double figure of eight knot to your harness every 6–7m in case the ascender fails.
- When bypassing a knot, clip a third sling above it before detaching etriers.
- Traverses are best aided across (sliding the ascenders ahead of you, but not weighted), because of the potential pendulums between pieces when ascending and the outward pull on gear.
- If the rope traverses a short distance or runs diagonally, clip a krab from the rear of the ascender to the rope to prevent it popping off the rope.
- It is important to tie off the climbing rope to your harness frequently.
- If there is a long span of rope between placements, lower yourself across. Thread a sling through the pendulum point and then thread a bight of rope from the harness through the sling. Clip this to a locking krab on your harness belay loop. Pull up the slack so that your weight is transferred on to the bight. Unclip the lead rope from the pendulum point and strip the krabs from the anchor. Lower yourself back into jumaring line. Unclip the bight of rope from your harness and pull it through the pendulum point.
- Mashies are best left in place, but tug a few times if you need to remove them and inspect each one carefully before using again. If the wire is stripped from the mashey, take the time to clean the head from the crack so others can use the placement.
- When you remove gear, clip into it with an old sling so as not to lose it.

AID CLIMBING

FIXED ROPES (Fig. 70)

Used when you reach a bivvy ledge and want to climb several further pitches. The ropes are then fixed to allow you to reach your high point the next day. Use a figure of nine knot on the anchor, because it easier to undo.

To prevent the rope being blown around, pull it taut and anchor it at the bottom – it can be loosened for ascending – see Fixed lines in *Rucksack Guide: Mountaineering in remote areas of the world* (2009).

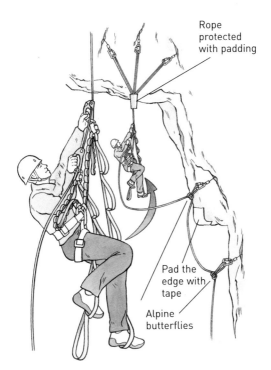

Rope protected with padding

Pad the edge with tape

Alpine butterflies

Fig. 70 *Fixed ropes*

Strength and stamina undoubtedly become more important as you climb harder routes, but the best way to become a better climber is to improve movement skills. Learning good movement at the start of your climbing career is vital, because bad movement patterns, once ingrained, are more difficult to overcome. Do not expect immediate success; learning the infinite variety of movements required to be a good rock climber, and making them automatic even under stress, takes practice and time.

Note: Do not practice the exercises in this section when you are at your limit or tired.

WHERE TO LEARN MOVEMENT

Climbing is an open skill and not a closed skill like a golf swing; you are trying to introduce rules for movement that the brain can select automatically, even under stress.

Learning movement is best done in a safe environment where you can focus. The best climbers practice on a variety of rock types, however, climbing walls are effective, as long as you understand the disadvantages:

● You don't necessarily become good at movement outdoors. Climbers moving from indoors to outdoors are strong, but rarely have the range of subtle techniques needed to climb on real rock and are poor at finding resting positions.

● Modern climbing walls rarely have the features of outside climbs, such as jam cracks, arêtes, slabs and corners.

● Poor route-setters design routes so that 'ape index' (the relationship between arm span and body height) is the limiting factor to success.

● Reaching the top often depends more on your levels of strength and endurance, rather than a wide repertoire of movement skills.

THE BENEFITS OF LEARNING GOOD MOVEMENT

- Your movements become more accurate and more consistent.
- You use less energy.
- You are able to anticipate movements early.
- Your confidence grows.
- You will climb harder routes with ease and in style.

PRE- AND POST-CLIMBING

Before climbing warm up to get the blood flowing, move your joints to lubricate them and do some easy climbing to wake up the brain-muscle link. After a climb, make sure to warm down and stretch properly.

SPOTTING

Spotting is the ability to limit injury to a falling climber while bouldering. Spotters do not catch falling climbers; they steer them to the best landing, slow them down and minimise the number of body parts hitting the ground. The size and skill of the spotter, the landing quality, plus the height above the ground all determine the seriousness of the 'boulder problem'.

- Big people are the best spotters, but are the hardest to spot; consider using two spotters if the climber is large.
- Correctly positioned bouldering mats can help to prevent injury, but may tempt you to go higher.
- On a steep boulder problem it is more effective to grab the sides of the climber's back just below the armpits and swing them back to a feet-first landing.
- On steep, high problems spot the climber's hips and steer them to a feet-first landing. Do not grab them too low, causing them to topple backwards.

You have four limbs equally capable of pushing and pulling, but it is your hips that place your centre of gravity (COG) in the best position, allowing all the other parts to be placed effectively. The steeper the rock, the more important the hips become.

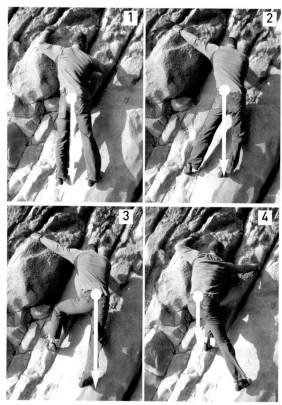

Fig. 71 *Put your COG in a balanced position by moving your hips to free a limb for movement: (1, 2) Lift the now-free leg, (3) Transfer your hips over the new foot placement (4).*

GENERAL EXERCISES

- **Move your hips** Try to take each limb, then combinations of two limbs, off the wall while adjusting your hips to stay in balance.

- **Use a balance beam** Bend, twist, turn sideways, dip your upper body and move your hips around. Use your leg as an outrigger, swinging forwards, backwards and sideways. Close your eyes, feeling the pressure in your legs and feet.

- **Climb smoothly** If you are snatching for footholds or handholds have you transferred your COG to find the most stable position? Compare climbing slowly and gracefully like a ballerina with climbing like a gorilla.

- **Study the rock** Design your own boulder problems. Mark holds with chalk and try it with a partner.

(A) Poor weight distribution

(B) Good weight distribution

Fig. 72 *Don't stretch for handholds (A). Keep your hips away from the rock on easier angled climbs and use your feet to gain height (B).*

It is important not to stretch for holds, therefore over-extending. Do not move your hands above the line of your head and move your feet twice before your hands, which enables you to reach further.

EDGING AND SMEARING FEET

1) Edging Keep the foot still, using the ankle as a hinge to prevent the upper body moving. Use the inside and outside edge of your feet. When using the outside edge of the toes, imagine they are being curled over the foothold. Do not place your foot deep into large holes, as it will force the lower leg outward, upsetting balance.

2) Smearing Place as much rubber as possible in contact with the rock. The steeper the rock, the more your hips must move away from it to direct the forces to your feet, or the harder your feet must push.

- Examine the rock in detail and try to stand on the smallest smears and edges you can find.
- Climb slowly, with no noise. Noisy footwork indicates that you are not climbing with precision. To improve, hover your foot over each hold for a few seconds before placing it. Remove and try to reposition it with your eyes closed.

Fig. 73 (1) Edging (2) Smearing

USE FEET IMAGINATIVELY

Take the strain off your arms with your feet; lock your toes in a horizontal crack, weight the heel and jam it in place. Use your heel to hook holds. Place your foot sideways in wider cracks.

ROCKOVERS

Rockovers highlight the importance of climbing smoothly, completing each move so that your centre of gravity is transferred completely over the new foot.

Fig. 74 Squat and use your legs to push rather than pulling with your arms:
(1) Move your hips over one leg
(2) Squat on to a straight arm
(3) Place the foot on to a new foothold
(4) Drive upwards with the lower leg and smoothly move your hip over it. Your trailing leg may leave the rock completely; let it hang in whichever position keeps you in balance ready for the next move.

On narrow holds keep your fingers together; if there is not room for all of them, give priority to the stronger middle and ring finger and curl the others up to optimise the muscle/tendon system.

THE FOUR MAIN HOLDS

1 The open hand (extended) grip
The least stressful on joints and tendons, but the most strenuous to use. Allows you to reach further and is often used on rounded holds, layaways and undercut moves.

2 The open crimp Bend the second finger joints at 90 degrees. The thumb is sometimes pinched.

3 The closed crimp The thumb backs up the next two fingers. Forces are concentrated in the fingertips, making it useful on very tiny holds. Keep the thumb close to the rock to reduce leverage. It is the easiest way to damage your fingers, because the second joint is contracted to its limit (consider taping your fingers).

4 The pinch grip Use as much of the thumb as possible and keep your palm close to the rock to reduce leverage.

Fig. 75 (1) Open hand grip (2) Open crimp (3) Closed crimp (4) Pinch grip

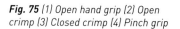

The structure of the rock dictates how your body can use holds:

LAYBACK/LIEBACK
This requires a keen awareness of your hip position. Laybacks are found anywhere where your body is to the side of your limbs, not just in corners. Practice on an arête or a single line of holds. Keep feet low – the steeper the rock, the higher your feet must be. Keep your arms straight, the hand nearest the rock should be highest. You can shuffle the hands and feet.

BRIDGING
When the rock is blank, only pressure through your feet and your arms keeps you in place. Bridge a corner without using footholds, try the opposite bridge with no handholds, then try to do it without hands or feet on positive holds.

*Fig. 76 Left: A classic layback position **Right**: Bridging can turn a strenuous position into a rest.*

CHIMNEYING
A chimney is a crack big enough for the body to fit into. Use your hands to push the back away and up, but not too far, or your feet may skid away.

> **FINGER TAPING**
>
> To prevent injuries, tape rings of 0.5–0.75in tape on either side of the finger joints. The 'X' method supports more of the finger: take a turn around the base of the finger; cross under the finger and take a turn around the middle of the finger; cross back and take another turn.

MANTLESHELF
The ability to gain a ledge without holds. Select the best part of a large hold or top of a boulder. Walk your feet up until your arms are almost straight. Step up, placing one foot on to the mantle. Turn one or both hands inwards to push and balance upwards. It is better to push down with the hand opposite the raised foot.

Fig. 77 Left: Chimneying Right: Mantleshelf

SIDE PULLS AND UNDERCLINGS

Undercling holds allow the feet to be moved higher, enabling you to reach further. The left/right rule of flagging is essential for performing side pull and undercling movements effectively, because you must use the outside edge of the foot opposite the handhold you are using. This allows the hip opposite the pulling hand to twist into the wall.

GASTON OR COMICI

Can be done with one or both hands. Pull hands in opposite directions to each other as if you are trying to open a lift door. Moving from this position usually requires leaning your hips to one side. The opposite can also be done by pulling or squeezing both sides of a large block.

Fig. 78 Left: Side pulls Right: Gaston/Comici technique

MOVE YOUR HIPS

On vertical rock bring your hips out when you move your feet, and back in when you move your hands. Swap or swivel feet to allow your body to twist to reach handholds (see *Mountaineering*, 2008).

THE LEFT/RIGHT RULE

On steep walls twisting your hips into the wall and working in a diagonal is more stable and creates a strength advantage when combined with twist locking, because it uses the chest muscles. On an overhanging wall try moving left arm and left leg then right arm and right leg, then try a diagonal combination – imagine the diagonal limbs are joined by a piece of elastic; as one limb moves, the opposite moves with it.

TWIST LOCKS

Combining twisting the hips with the left/right rule creates a very strong, stable position. Twist into a left-arm lock off, standing on the outside edge of the right foot (the body will then face left). The other foot may be inside flagging, or dangling in space. Vary the position of your head and see what effect it has. Twisting also allows you to reach further.

Fig. 79 The left/right rule

FLAGGING, BACK STEPPING AND KNEE DROPPING (EGYPTIANS)

- **Flagging** When only one arm and leg is in contact with the rock, use the other as a counterbalance (1). On a steep route try to remove both left hand and foot off. The only way to prevent a barn door is to flag. Inside flagging with a twist lock helps to avoid switching feet on an insecure foothold (2).

- **Back stepping** Attain a bridged position between two holds, rotate sideways and step the outside edge of the foot on to a hold behind you. Keep your weight over the new hold, using the arm on the same side of the body as the back-stepped foot to reach.

- **Knee drops** Drop your knee and torso so the rear knee bends downwards. Keep your weight over the foot that has been back-stepped by placing the dropped knee under your buttocks, which allows you to squat and secure a rest position.

Left arm

Right foot

Fig. 80 Top: Outside flagging
Centre: Inside flagging
Bottom: Back stepping and knee dropping

Down climb to a rest spot then work out the moves, rather than become pumped hanging on at the crux. Efficient rest positions depend on three factors:

- **Body position** Keep your centre of gravity over your feet.
- **Fitness** The ability of the body to avoid the dreaded pump.
- **State of mind** How many times have you been 'gripped' while placing a runner only to find you are relaxed as soon as it is in place?

USING THE BODY FOR WEDGING AND HOOKING

- Place your backside on or lay the forearm across a hold.
- Hook your chin over an edge.
- Use your hand as a third foothold.
- A toe hook helps balance and keeps your weight over your feet.
- Use a 'thumb catch': lay or hook the thumb over an edge and wriggle the fingers.
- Alternate fingers and hands on the hold on small edges.
- 'Match' hands on the holds by making space between the fingers for the other hand.
- Push your chest and stem out into a corner.
- 'Chicken wing' by putting arms or elbows against the walls.
- Use knee bars: jam a knee against a hold or roof and push with the foot to wedge it in place.

RESTING THE ARMS

Keep your arms low to allow the blood to flow to your hands more easily. If your arms are above head-height, grip the rock with minimal force. Keep your arms straight ('monkey hanging') by bridging or sinking into 'a squat' (frogging) or twist and knee drop.

Try to climb a route with big holds using straight arms. Use the arms as a lever and the shoulder as a hinge, push with the legs – as the hips are rolled towards the straight arm the body twists and increases the reach.

BREATHING/SHAKING OUT

Breathe slowly and deeply when resting and breathe out when undertaking a strenuous move. If your arms are pumped, hold them low to allow the blood to drain the lactic acid away, then shake them high and let them gently drop. Push your palm against a hold to stretch your forearms.

DYNAMIC MOVEMENTS (DYNOS)

A Dyno is a controlled dash for a hold.

- Bend the knees and sink down, breathing out as you push up.
- On overhanging walls keep your arms straight, but on less steep walls pull with your arms as you move upwards to keep your hips into the wall.
- Don't bounce: crouch once and then do it.
- Consider which hand is doing the holding and which hand the propelling.
- Try to grasp the hold at the highest point of the move-ment when the body is motionless (the 'dead point').

Fig. 81 *There are times when you may require momentum to 'snatch' for a higher hold.*

Crack climbing can feel unnatural and even painful when done poorly; tape your hands and fingers to avoid injury.

HAND SEQUENCE

Jamming face cracks requires one hand to cross over the other; corner cracks require the hands to be shuffled, because the body can't be twisted as easily. Which hand stays on top depends on which shoulder is against the rock. Shuffling is rarely used in straight finger cracks, because it feels more secure to alternately place one above the other.

FINGER JAMMING

Put the top hand in thumb down; the lower hand in thumb up or down. Placing the thumb down creates leverage, which increases as you move higher. Placing the thumb up allows a further reach to be made for the next placement.

HAND JAMMING

The thumb can be up or down depending on the crack. Push the fingers and the palm of the hand against one side of the crack and the knuckles against the other; the hand will jam. On wider cracks place the thumb into the palm of the hand giving it more bulk. When it widens, form a fist shape and jam this in place.

Fig. 82 *Finger jam: press the thumb against the crack (a sprag)*

Fig. 83 *Hand jams start when the hand slides in as far as the wrist and end as a fist jam as the crack widens.*

USING YOUR FEET IN CRACKS

On pure crack climbs your feet may be twisted and contorted so they also cam in the crack. A few short movements are better than one long one.

OFF-WIDTHS

Off-widths are full body jams, where the arms and legs are used to apply pressure to opposite sides of the crack. Stick an arm in until it is just past the shoulder, and bend at the elbow, pressing the palm against one side and the elbow and shoulder against the other. The outside arm pulls on the outside edge of the crack at neck level. Do not let you arms get too high above your head, otherwise they will become pumped. Jam the legs by locking a foot against one wall and the knee against the other or, if it is small enough, by jamming the heel and toe into the crack. The most important thing is to maintain a rhythm and use momentum gained from the push or pull to initiate the next.

You may never have the mental control of a top climber, because of influences on you growing up and factors dictated by your genes, but there are things you can do to increase confidence in your climbing. Releasing tension through relaxation, focusing and improving your self-belief can channel 'flight or fight' syndrome into your climbing and you enter what some climbers call 'the zone' (the moment where you are aware of nothing but the movement).

USING IMAGERY TO IMPROVE YOUR MOVEMENT SKILLS

Studies have demonstrated that the brain is not always capable of distinguishing between something that actually happened and something that was imagined. Picturing yourself executing a perfect performance can therefore help your brain to enhance that skill. Using imagery is an acquired skill, requiring the same effort and discipline as working out, and takes time to learn.

- Relax, then concentrate and stay alert. Look at a problem or climb and imagine yourself or someone else doing it. Use all of your senses, not just sight. Try to imagine scenes in explicit detail; where will your hands go? Which way will your body shift? Feel yourself doing the moves.

- Be realistic – it won't help imagining yourself climbing the hardest route in the world! Create positive images of dealing with problems on a climb and eliminate images of failure. Work daily in 5–10 minute sessions to change negative images to positive ones. If you get bored, stop.

RELAXATION

Relaxation allows you to regain your physical, mental and emotional energy. It is different to focusing (concentration), which is a withdrawal of attention from irrelevant factors. There are two levels; total and momentary. Do total relaxation after, rather than before, a climb, otherwise you may become too relaxed. Momentary relaxation is best done prior to a warm up or imagery, when you are anxious, before a climb and when learning a new skill. Most techniques calm you by occupying the mind with something simple.

- Go to a quiet place with no distractions. Lying down helps you to reach a deeper state of relaxation, but it may reduce the alertness you need to climb.

- Take each muscle group in sequence, tense and then release it. Be aware of the difference in tension. Alternatively, try imagining that you are filled up with liquid – let it flow out of your toes very slowly until empty.

FOCUSING

During stress the body narrows it's attention to what is essential for survival. This can have unfortunate consequences: we tend to become obsessed with handholds instead of footholds and style deteriorates; we narrow our focus to holds immediately in front of us and fail to see crucial holds on the periphery; we search for gear instead of making the moves. Focusing distances you from worries or distractions beyond your control and helps you stay in the present. There are many methods for practising concentration:

- Sit in a chair and place a photograph of climbing in front of you. Relax and sit for five minutes without moving, noticing as many qualities of the photograph as you can. If your mind wanders, start again.

- Practice on easy climbs by focusing on one aspect of movement such as using the minimum of grip on hand placements. If your attention wanders, refocus.

- Go through possible problems and develop solutions for each one.

- Psyche up by imagining how it feels to stand at the top of the route. Relax and talk to yourself, inwardly or outwardly.

TALKING POSITIVELY

Self-belief is thinking you can do what you have set out to do. It is possible to train yourself to think positively, thereby allowing you to focus and relax. Positive self-talk or affirmations reinforce a positive image, e.g. 'I can get up this route', 'The crux is hard, but it's well protected', 'I've climbed much harder on a top rope'.

Negative self-talk has a negative effect on self-image and induces anxiety, e.g. 'It's too hard', 'The crux is steep and I may not get protection in', 'I found an easier route than this desperate a few months ago'. Friends can help by offering positive encouragement i.e. 'You can climb it!' rather than 'Give it a go', which gives an opt out.

STAYING CALM BEFORE THE CLIMB

- The worst fear is the unknown. Start by knowing the climbing environment, gradually increasing your experience and knowledge. Understand ropework; how to escape from a route; how to survive a storm and avoid avalanches.

- Some crags are intimidating. Climb a problem or route you can flow up before trying a route that is going to push you. Concentrate on the positive feelings that success evokes. Top-rope a route or abseil down to place runners prior to leading.

- Rehearse the moves and expect success.

- Don't venture on your hardest lead when you're not happy or fatigued.

- Do you really want to climb the route? Motivation to climb is personal, but is affected by outside factors; a good friend can help by encouraging you (confidence takes a long time to enhance, but seconds to destroy). Mix with better climbers; it is amazing how you pick up their positive vibes.

- Forget previous failures, viewing each route as a new chapter in your climbing career.

- Break the route into sections or islands of retreat and accept using aid and rests on routes that are difficult.
- Are your thoughts positive or negative? Relax and create a positive image of yourself climbing the route.
- Slow everything down. Take your time tying in and putting your shoes on, using it as a time to relax.
- Build confidence by using a belayer you trust.

STAYING CALM DURING THE CLIMB
- Strive for elegance.
- Become calm at rests.
- Double your runners up.
- Fool yourself and climb as if the holds are big.
- Down climb if in trouble.
- Talk positively.
- Breathe in a controlled manner. When in doubt, breathe out.
- Distract yourself – create an affirmation to focus your mind on a particular aspect of climbing, e.g. silent climbing (use your feet to help you to calm down and release your grip on the rock).
- Try to relax on the route – close your eyes, breathe and transport yourself to a desert island or somewhere quiet.

MOUNTAIN WALKING AND TREKKING

This book is ideal for novices and experienced walkers alike, including everything you need to know about navigating hills and mountains. It includes a section on weather, from interpreting charts to dealing with a thunderstorm, tells you how to prepare for your trek, including packing your rucksack, demystifies the art of scrambling and climbing Via ferrata safely.

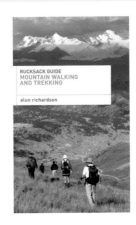

RUCKSACK GUIDE
MOUNTAIN WALKING
AND TREKKING

alun richardson

MOUNTAINEERING IN REMOTE AREAS OF THE WORLD

This is the essential handbook for planning and undertaking mountaineering expeditions around the world. It offers concise guidance, including where to go and when, advice on dangerous animals and minimising your impact on the environment, and dealing with extreme situations.

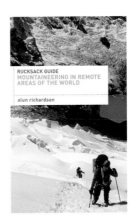

RUCKSACK GUIDE
MOUNTAINEERING IN REMOTE
AREAS OF THE WORLD

alun richardson

ALPINISM

Venturing to the Alps for the first time can be daunting. This volume covers everything you need to know about ascending these magnificent mountains, in summer and winter.

SKI MOUNTAINEERING AND SNOWSHOEING

Mountaineering on skis or snowshoes requires the ability to ski off-piste, good navigation skills, and awareness of the risks of the mountain environment in winter – you will find all of the above and more covered in this handbook.

WINTER MOUNTAINEERING

Mountains transformed by snow and ice are a world apart from lush summer slopes. This volume provides you with the techniques to explore wintry plateaus, tackle rocky ridges and ascend snowy slopes.